Portraits of Flowers

Portraits of Flowers

Ann Reilly

PORTLAND HOUSE
Distributed by Outlet Book Company, Inc.
A Random House Company
225 Park Avenue South
New York, New York 10003

This 1990 edition published by Portland House,
distributed by Outlet Book Company, Inc.,
a Random House Company,
225 Park Avenue South, New York, New York 10003

ISBN 0-517-05073-0
8 7 6 5 4 3 2 1

Printed and bound in Spain

For rights information about the photographs in
this book please contact:

The Image Bank
111 Fifth Avenue, New York, NY 10003

Writer: Ann Reilly

Producer: Solomon M. Skolnick
Designer: Ann-Louise Lipman
Editor: Sara Colacurto
Production: Valerie Zars
Senior Picture Researcher: Edward Douglas
Editorial Assistant: Carol Raguso
Project Picture Researcher: Robert V. Hale

i. *Common zinnia,* Zinnia elegans.
ii. *Dahlia, Doris Day.*
iii. *Delphinium,* Consolida ambigua.
iv. *(top) Common bearded iris,* Iris X germanica.
iv. *(bottom) Madonna lilies,* Lilium candidum.
v. *(top) Red petunia,* Petunia X hybrida.
v. *(bottom) White petunia,* Petunia X hybrida.
vi. *Hybrid tea rose.*

Table of Contents

The garden. It is older than human life—many believe that man first lived in the Garden of Eden. But cultivated gardens did not appear until early man stopped his nomadic wanderings to settle in one location. While most of these gardens were dedicated to the production of food, there is no doubt that some also provided food for the soul.

The ancient roots of today's garden branch out in many directions. Many of the blooms in modern flower beds and borders were known before Christ. Excavation of Egyptian tombs has shown that flowers and gardens were an important part of this ancient civilization. About 605 B.C., in the valley of the Tigris and Euphrates Rivers, Nebuchadnezzar created the Hanging Gardens of Babylon, one of the Seven Wonders of the Ancient World. When the Persians conquered Egypt in 525 B.C., they borrowed the principles of the formal Egyptian gardens, spreading them across Asia Minor. The Persians loved flowers and even believed that their Heaven was a garden. It is thought that container gardening started in Greece, and in Rome, gardens were one source of Roman pleasure.

Early western civilizations spread the love of gardening as far east as India, into northern Africa, and throughout the Mediterranean. Different styles of gardening developed as divergent cultures emerged. In the Middle Ages, gardens were kept in monasteries. Later, they were developed during the glorious Renaissance. Some plants and flowers were discovered in the New World during the sixteenth and seventeenth centuries' Age of Exploration. These were introduced to

Europe, where they were cultivated, improved, and returned to American shores by the early settlers. Once travel became common between east and west, a plethora of plants filled nurseries and gardens. Perhaps the most spectacular gardens were cultivated in seventeenth- and eighteenth-century France, but by the mid-eighteenth century, England was the center of the gardening world.

Concurrent with the development of gardens in the western world, came the development of the art of gardening in China. Chinese gardening principles were subsequently introduced to Japan, most likely by way of Korea, and flowers and gardens became rich in symbolism. Europeans first learned of these gardens, especially those of the thirteenth-century Mongol emperor Kublai Kahn, from the Venetian traveler Marco Polo. During the seventeenth century, when trade routes were opened between the east and west, the influence of Oriental gardens and plants became apparent in Occidental gardens.

Modern communications and transportation have made the world smaller, and the gardening world has not been immune to their influences. Gardening styles and garden plants have evolved significantly. While different styles of gardening exist, today's gardens are more universal than ever before. It is this universality of the plant world that helps to draw different cultures together. It is the plant world that knows no social barriers, existing to bring superb beauty and joy to all mankind.

CHERRY

Cherry blossom time...the time of year when the skies are no longer gray, the air no longer cold...a time when life is renewed and the spirits are lifted. It is no wonder that cherry blossom festivals are held throughout the world, the most famous U.S. festival being held in Washington D.C. each April.

Cherry trees are divided into two categories, those grown for fruit and those grown for ornamental purposes. Most, but not all, of those grown for fruit are native to Europe, whereas most of those grown for ornament are from Asia. Cherry trees are widespread and native to all of the Northern Hemisphere.

Nearly all ornamental cherry trees are sterile, which is why, usually, they do not set fruit. Some do bear fruit, but it is either inconspicuous, inedible, or both. However, the clouds of soft pink and white flowers that herald the arrival of spring make the planting of these sterile cherry trees universal. Most of the cherry trees in Washington, D.C., are Yoshino cherry trees, *Prunus X yedoensis,* a gift to the U.S. from the government of Japan. Their semi-double flowers are produced in billowing masses and bring tens of thousands of tourists to Washington's Tidal Basin each spring. *P. serrulata* is Washington's other variety of cherry tree.

The Yoshino cherry tree is a complex hybrid of *P. serrulata* and *P. subhirtella.* The former, a Japanese flowering cherry tree, has pink or white flowers, and its variety, Kwanzan, which has stiff, upright, spreading branches filled with powderpuffs of double pink flowers, is one of the best known and most widely planted cherry trees. Of ancient origin, Japanese flowering cherry trees were the first to be brought to Europe from the Orient, in 1822. Another variety of *P. serrulata,* known as Hill Cherry, is the most adored tree in Japan; it is one that has inspired both poets and artists.

P. subhirtella, the Higan cherry tree—and especially its variety, Pendula—has graceful, arching branches that form a sheer curtain of delicate double pink flowers that bloom with forsythia and daffodils. The Sargent cherry, *P. sargentii,* is another Asian contribution to American gardens; it is one of the oldest varieties of cherry trees. *P. sargentii,* has red flowers and a beautiful, glossy red bark.

The most widespread cherry tree native to North America is *P. virginiana,* known as chokecherry for the bitter taste of its fruits. It grows in large thickets and is used to stabilize soil.

The edible cherries are divided into two categories: sweet cherries, which are usually eaten fresh, and sour cherries, which are used in pies, preserves, and sauces. Because of their cultural requirements and susceptibility to late spring frosts, sweet cherries, *P. avium,* are grown primarily in the Pacific Northwest whereas sour cherries, *P. cerasus,* which are bitter in taste, are grown along the Great Lakes.

There are also wild forms of sweet cherries that grow across the U.S. and Europe, as well as other cherry trees with edible fruit. These include *P. tomentosa,* the Nanking cherry tree, a low-growing, multistemmed plant from central Asia that is often used as a hedge; *P. pumila,* the sand cherry tree, native to eastern U.S. beaches; and *P. besseyi,* the western sand cherry tree, a native of the central U.S.

In addition to dessert and other culinary uses, cherries are used in making alcoholic beverages. Kirschwasser is made along the upper Rhine from a wild, sweet black cherry. Cherry Heering is a similar drink traditional in Scandinavia. The marasca cherry from Yugoslavia is used to make maraschino cherries and a liqueur also called maraschino. The sloe berry, *P. spinosa,* which is used to flavor sloe gin, is a close relative of the cherry. These berries are also used in preserves and wine, and the wood is used to make blackthorn sticks and Irish shillelaghs.

Cherry wood, especially from the black cherry tree, *P. serotina,* is a prized wood used in furniture and cabinetmaking. Native to eastern North America, the black cherry tree is a thorn in the sides of dairy farmers, as its fallen leaves decompose into glucose and cyanic acid, poisoning the cattle that eat them. The bark, however, has been used safely and efficiently in cough medicines.

The wood of the bird cherry tree, *P. padus,* has been used for furniture, boat building, and interior work. This cherry tree has white, almond-scented flowers and, like many other cherry trees, an attractive, peeling bark.

Cherry trees are members of the rose family and are closely related to plums, apricots, almonds, nectarines and peaches. The genus name for all of these, *Prunus,* is derived from the Latin word *prunum* and the Greek word *proumnon,* which mean "plum."

The cherry has also had an influence on the English language. The globular red firecracker associated with the Fourth of July is called a cherry bomb. The movable crane that holds a worker in a bucket on the end of a boom is called a cherry picker; it was first used for exactly that purpose, and one of the smallest clams is called a cherrystone.

Although cherry blossoms are either white, red, or pink, it was the pink tones that were memorialized in the song of the 1950's that stated "and that is why the poets always write, when your true lover comes your way, it's cherry pink and apple blossom white, the poets say."

Chuh-sien, which means the city of chrysanthemums.

The perennial *Chrysanthemum X morifolium,* the mum of the florist shop and garden, is a complex hybrid that is assumed to have originated in China. Mums were favorites of the noble class and, until the revolution in China, those who were not of "blue blood" were not allowed to grow them in their gardens. The Chinese used mums in teas and in wine to increase vitality and to prolong life, and still consider the mum a symbol of rest and ease.

Mums were introduced into Japan around the fourth century; the seeds came from China through Korea. There is a legend that states that Japan was founded when two dozen young men and women sailed from China to find an herb that would keep them forever young. They took chrysanthemums with them to trade for this herb, but never reached their destination; they were ship-wrecked instead. They planted the mums on the uninhabited island and stayed there to build the empire.

In 910, Japan held its first Imperial Chrysanthemum Show and declared the mum its national flower, which it remains today. The imperial coat of arms shows a 16-petaled golden chrysanthemum, considered a sign of long life and happiness. It is the Japanese floral symbol for September. To this day, they use the leaves and flowers of crown daisy, *C. coronarium,* in salads and other recipes.

Oriental mums first reached Europe in 1688, but they were not received with enthusiasm. It was not until the early nineteenth century when new varieties arrived from China that hybridizing began. In 1843, when the Royal Horticultural Society in England collected yet new strains of *C. X morifolium* from China, interest in the mum began to pick up. Flowers from Japan were introduced in the 1860's, and crossbreeding produced a wide array of plant sizes and flower forms. The French especially liked the small-flowered varieties because such flowers reminded them of the small pompons that were found on their sailors' hats.

The chrysanthemum of today can range from the ground-hugging cushion mums to the tall, stately plants that produce blooms the size of dinner plates. The color range has expanded to include all colors except true blue, and many flowers are interestingly two-toned. Flower forms range from singles to doubles, and include such unique varieties as anemone, pompon, incurved, reflexed, spider, spoon, and other decorative types.

The U.S. first received the mum in 1798, and as many as 40 different varieties were known by 1850. The Chrysanthemum Society of America was established in 1900, and the first Mum Show was held in Chicago in 1902.

Once horticulturists understood the principle of photoperiodism, mum flowers were available all year. The mum blooms naturally when the day is shorter than 14½ hours. When plants are covered with black cloth or plastic for at least 9½ hours they will set buds, which will open if they receive 10½ hours of darkness.

CHRYSANTHEMUM

Chrysanthemums, which are members of the daisy family, are very old plants; Confucius wrote about them in 500 B.C. In ancient China, botanist T'ao Ming-yang developed so many new strains of chrysanthemums that they became a great attraction, and people would travel from far distances to see them. His village was renamed

Many of the recent introductions of garden mums belong to the *C. zawadskii* species and are called Korean chrysanthemums. Native to the Far East, they have been hybridized with *C. X morifolium* to produce very hardy plants with single and double flowers in many colors.

One of the relatives of the garden mum, the oxeye daisy, *C. levcanthemum,* although native to Europe and Asia, has become a common wildflower across the U.S., Canada, and Mexico. The oxeye daisy is also known as Marguerite. It was named after Margaret of Anjou, Queen of Henry VI, who took the flower as her emblem in 1445. It was popular in Europe as a meadow and garden plant for several hundred years until interest in *C. maximum* and its hybrid *C. X superbum,* the Shasta daisy, gave the Marguerite a back-seat position. The Shasta daisy is a more robust plant that has single or double white daisy-like flowers with golden centers that bloom all summer.

To add to the confusion, another species of annual chrysanthemum, *C. frutescens,* is also called Marguerite. Native to the Canary Islands, it is sometimes called Paris Daisy as well because it was introduced to France in the late sixteenth century. This flower, with single and double forms in white, pink, and yellow, is common in florists' spring and summer arrangements.

Another close relative is the feverfew, *C. parthenium,* a European native with curled, pungent leaves and tiny, white, buttonlike flowers. It is called feverfew because it was used as a tonic to combat fevers; it was also used in potpourri to repel insects. Costmary, *C. balsamita,* was used in beer before brewers began using hops. Costmary was called Bibleleaf in early American days, because churchgoers used it as a bookmark and nibbled on it to stay awake during services. The leaves have a balsam flavor and are used in salads, stews, or soup.

The painted daisy, *C. coccieum,* is a spring-blooming perennial in pretty pastel shades. It is the source of the natural insecticide, pyrethrum, and is cultivated in East Africa for that reason. Pyrethrum is also derived from *C. ciner ariifolium.*

The name chrysanthemum is derived from two Latin words meaning "yellow" and "flower." Chrysanthemum plants are quite aromatic. The petals are edible and tasty and are often used in soups, teas, and as a garnish on salads, fruit dishes, and cheese dips.

CROCUS

Growing from a bulblike structure called a corm, the crocus is native to Spain, North Africa, China, the Mediterranean, Turkey, and the Balkan Peninsula. Crocuses are ancient plants dating back to 1500 B.C. Artifacts from that period have been found that list the medicinal value of the crocus.

Many myths and legends are associated with the crocus. One tells of Crocus, son of Europa, accidentally killed by Mercury, who then transformed him into the flower. Another states that Crocus fell in love with Smilax, who spurned his attentions. The gods, in an attempt to help him recover from his distress, turned him into the flower, and turned Smilax into a yew.

Homer wrote that crocus was used to make the marriage bed for Zeus and Hera. The Greeks used crocus petals as decorations for parties and believed that it inspired love. The first-century Roman writer, Pliny, suggested wearing crocus around the neck to dispel the odor of wine and to prevent drunkenness.

The oldest cultivated crocus, and one of the oldest of all cultivated plants, is *Crocus sativus,* from which the herb saffron comes. It is believed that the Mongols carried it into China and the Romans into northern Europe.

It is the orange or red stigma—the tip of the female part of the crocus flower—that is used to make saffron, which is very expensive. It takes several hundred plants to harvest enough saffron to fill a tiny container, several thousand plants to make an ounce; and the price of saffron—about $3,000 a pound—has led many to turn to safflower, *Carthamus tinctoria,* as a substitute. Known as false saffron, safflower has deep yellow to orange flowers that when crushed and dried are very similar to saffron. Saffron was used as a dye for church vestments and gold cloth worn by the wealthy in Europe and Asia through at least the sixteenth century. It was also a yellow coloring and flavoring for food, especially rice, cake, and bread. Saffron is a fall-blooming crocus with white or lavender flowers.

The name crocus comes from the Greek *krokos,* which means "thread" and refers to the threadlike stigma of the crocus flower. The word saffron is derived from the Spanish word *acafron* and the Arabic word *sahafarn,* both of which also mean thread.

Crocuses, particularly saffron, were thought to have medicinal qualities. The English believed saffron would cure rheumatism, and it was also believed to strengthen teeth. Saffron tea has been recommended for fevers and treating measles.

The best-known garden crocus, sometimes called Dutch crocus, is the spring-flowering hybrid of *C. vernus.* One of the earliest decorative species in cultivation, it has large flowers of purple, blue, white, or yellow, often solid-colored, often striped. Although the large-flowered Dutch hybrid crocus is favored by many gardeners, there are also a number of other crocus species that deserve a place in the garden. Most bloom earlier and are longer lasting than Dutch crocuses.

C. angustifolius, cloth-of-gold crocus, is orange-gold with a dark brown center stripe that was known by at least the sixteenth century. *C. biflorus,* Scotch crocus, bears flowers that may be white or lilac and that can be striped or veined with purplish blue; it has a yellow throat. These flowers appear in very early spring and are native to southern Europe and Asia Minor, despite their name. *C. versicolor,* cloth-of-silver crocus, has spring-borne flowers that are purple on the outside and yellow or white on the inside.

C. chrysanthus bears fragrant, early blooming flowers that range from pale yellow to orange yellow and has hybrids of white or blue. *C. flavus* produces deep golden-yellow flowers that combine well with blue-flowered crocus. *C. imperati,* early crocus, bears flowers that are buff colored or yellow with purple stripes on the outside and bright purple inside. These flowers are very fragrant and appear in early spring. They were known before the mid-1600's and were at one time called Episcopalis. *C. tomasinianus,* which was discovered in the nineteenth century in Hungary and Bulgaria, has lilac to purple flowers with white throats.

Several crocuses in addition to *C. sativus* (saffron) are fall blooming. Among the fall-flowering crocuses are the star-shaped, fragrant, pinkish-purple *C. goulimyi,* a species that does well in frost-free areas (most crocuses need winter cold to grow well). *C. speciosus,* in gardens since the late nineteenth century, is a very showy fall-blooming species with violet-blue flowers and bright orange stigmas. It is one of the most reliable of the fall-flowering crocuses. A plant that looks amazingly like a crocus, but is not a crocus at all and is not even closely related, is *Colchicum autumnale.* Better known as autumn crocus, it is the source of the drug colchicine that is used to treat gout.

By the late sixteenth century, gardeners were selecting interesting crocus seedlings and collecting plants from the wild. Florists' crocuses in solid colors and striped shades of yellow, white, and purple were known by the seventeenth century. The Dutch led the industry in the eighteenth and nineteenth centuries and still produce most of the world's bulbs. Almost 450 million crocuses are exported from Holland each year, making it that country's fourth-largest crop.

DAFFODIL

Daffodils, which are in the genus *Narcissus,* are also steeped in ancient legends and lores. It is said that Pluto, god of the underworld, was in love with Demeter's daughter, Persephone and, to lure her to his land, asked his brother Zeus to create the daffodil. When Persephone went to gather flowers with her friends, she bypassed the roses, crocuses, violets, hyacinths, lilies, and irises to find out what this new and beautiful flower was. Approaching the daffodils, as Zeus knew she would, she was swept off her feet by Pluto, who sprang forth in his chariot from an opening in the earth. There are other variations to this story, one of which says that daffodil flowers nod their heads for the maiden's sorrow at being kidnapped by Pluto.

Legend also says that daffodils were consecrated to the Furies, who were supposed to have used them to stupefy those whom they wished to punish. Other ancient writers claimed that the sweet fragrance of the flowers led to hallucinations and that all daffodils belonged to Venus except the yellow ones, which belonged to Mars. The word narcissism, which means egocentrism or love of one's own body, comes from a story about a Greek youth who was too much in love with himself. The legend goes that Echo, a mountain nymph, was in love with Narcissus, but he was so vain that he did not notice. All he did was sit and look at his reflection in a pool of water. When Echo was spurned and left, leaving nothing behind but her voice, the gods were so angry that they changed Narcissus into a flower, destined to always nod at his own reflection in a pool of water.

The first written record of daffodils dates back to ancient times, to the Greek physician Dioscorides; the Roman scholar Pliny, who identified three different kinds of narcissi; and Theophrastus, who wrote about *poeticus* daffodils as early as 320 B.C. The tazetta daffodil was also known in ancient Egypt and Greece and eventually found its way to China and Japan, presumably along early trade routes. When it reached the Orient, it became known as the sacred lily of China and is still a symbol of purity and promise and the floral emblem of the Chinese New Year. In Japan, the daffodil is a symbol of joyousness and the emblem of formality.

Narcissus bulbs are poisonous, containing a chemical that paralyzes the heart and numbs the nervous system. Nevertheless, Galen, physician to the Roman gladiators, used the juice from the bulbs to heal cuts and wounds, a practice also carried out in medieval England.

The word narcissus comes from the Greek word *narkeo,* which means "to be stupefied," probably relating to the poisonous quality of the bulb. It is not known exactly how the word daffodil was derived. One thought is that Norman soldiers thought it was similar to the d'asphodel, a cousin of the lily, and that the name changed from d'asphodel to daffodil. Another stems from the Old English affodyle, which means "that which comes early." The jonquil was named after the Spanish word *juncas,* which means "rush," because its foliage resembles that of the rush plant.

The jonquil was a favorite of Queen Anne, who wove it into her laces and tapestries. Her love for jonquils further led her to establish Kensington Palace Gardens, the first public gardens in England. Daffodils were so popular in the Stuart court that the hillsides were being depleted of its blooms — hence came the first protective plant legislation. Traditionally in England, the first Sunday in April was Daffodil Sunday, when flowers were picked for patients at London hospitals.

Native to Europe, particularly Spain and Portugal, and to North Africa, the daffodil genus has a little more than two dozen species, one of which is the jonquil, another the trumpet daffodil — yet another popular plant for indoor forcing in winter. Because there are so many different flower forms of the daffodil, efforts have been made at a classification system. John Parkinson, the English horticulturist, devised the first system in 1629; he divided daffodils into "true" and "bastard" daffodils. Many other attempts followed; the most useful was adopted in 1909 by the Royal Horticultural Society of London. There have been five revisions since, most recently in 1977.

This classification system breaks the daffodil down into 12 divisions based on the size and shape of the corona, cup or trumpet (the central part of the flower), and the perianth (the petals surrounding the center). Perhaps the most well known is Division 1, the trumpet daffodil, which has one flower to a stem and the trumpet as long or longer than the perianth. Division 2, the large-cupped daffodil, is similar, but the cup is one-third to less than equal the length of the perianth. The small-cupped daffodil, Division 3, is also similar, but the cup is less than one-third the length of the perianth.

Double daffodils, a self-explanatory name, fall into Division 4. Those daffodils with more than one drooping flower with a re-flexed perianth are known as *triandrus,* Division 5; the *cyclamineus,* Division 6, also have reflexed petals, but the flower does not droop and blooms one to a stem. Both jonquils (Division 7) and tazetta (Division 8) daffodils have several flowers to a stem and are fragrant; the jonquils resemble trumpet daffodils and the tazettas have short cups. *Poeticus* (Division 9) have fragrant white petals and a small, flat cup. Number 10 is the only division that contains daffodils not created by man. These are species and wild forms. When the center is double for one-third of its length or more, it is a split corona daffodil (Division 11), and all those that don't

fall into the above categories are lumped into Division 12, miscellaneous.

The first written account of daffodils in modern times dates from 1548; many records appear about its being grown in Europe soon thereafter and in American gardens by the end of the 1700's. In the early 1800's, plant breeders began with a handful of wild daffodils, crossbreeding them and creating new forms. Over the years, breeders have achieved more than 24,000 named varieties (although some have been forever lost to the plant world). If you meet a serious collector, he or she will no doubt be a member of the American Daffodil Society. Organized in 1958, it now boasts thousands of members and presents hundreds of daffodil shows across the country from early March to mid-May, depending on the climate and the time of peak bloom. England's Daffodil Society dates back even further, to 1898.

True daffodil enthusiasts will literally go to the end of the earth for new varieties and empty their pocketbooks in the process. Some newly introduced bulbs with rare colors will change hands for over $100 for a single bulb. This is not a new phenomenon; Will Scarlet, the first breakthrough of red color in daffodils, was $50 a bulb when introduced in 1898, and the red Fortune, which sold for $75 a bulb when it was introduced in 1923, is now sold by the hundreds of tons each year at affordable prices.

Growing from a true bulb, the daffodil is certainly one of the most welcome signs of spring. There is nothing more breathtaking than a hillside of cheerful, golden trumpets swaying in the breeze as the first warm days of spring settle in. King Alfred, which is over a century old, is still the classic golden yellow daffodil. Other than golden yellow, daffodils can also have white, orange, or red in their coloration. Although some daffodils are called pink, such as the famous Mrs. R. O. Backhouse registered in 1923, they are not a true pink, but a yellow or salmon color with a pink tinge.

Although most daffodils are produced in Holland, where 4,000 acres are devoted to the crop, many are grown in the U.S. in the shadow of Mt. Rainier, Washington. The Puyallup Daffodil Festival held each year in late March culminates in the Grand Floral Parade and is billed as the third-largest floral parade in the country.

It is not surprising then that daffodils have often been lauded by the world's greatest writers. Many would agree with Mohammed that bread is but food for the body, whereas narcissus is food for the soul.

The beauty of the cherry blossom is one reason why visitors flock to Washington, D.C., every year in early spring — to soak up the spectacle of these trees, which are planted along the Tidal Basin.

Among the most graceful of cherry trees is the weeping cherry, Prunus subhirtella pendula, *whose branches, laden with tiny flowers, reach for the sky before gesturing towards the ground.*

Alfred Edward Housman (1859–1936) wrote of the cherry:

> Loveliest of trees, the cherry now
> Is hung with bloom along the bough.

Housman wrote again of cherries:

> And since to look at things in bloom
> Fifty springs are little room,
> About the woodlands I will go
> To see the cherry hung with snow.

*As a chrysanthemum opens to an early morning
autumn sun, its petals display the colors traditionally
associated with this brisk season and reflect the gold,
russets, and bronzes of the turning leaves.*

Preceding pages: *Spider mums intermingle with marigolds and dianthus in a late summer garden. At one time, mums did not bloom outdoors unless shaded until midfall. Today, thanks to modern plant breeding, mums can be in bloom by late summer.*

The stately chrysanthemum was first brought to the U.S. in 1798. It has been grown in Oriental gardens since at least the fifth century B.C. and possibly even earlier.

Although many flowers have daisylike blooms, some people feel that the single chrysanthemum epitomizes this type (Compositae) of flower. Other chrysanthemums have flowers described as "spoons," because the petals have small cups at the ends, and "anemones," because of their tufted centers.

The chrysanthemum Mirage is a type of mum known as a button mum, because, although they grow in giant clusters, the flowers are very tiny. They are similar to pompon mums, except that they are smaller.

The chrysanthemum Remarkable is
a form of mum known as decorative.
Its rich reddish-bronze petals hold
their color even in bright sun,
producing a remarkable outdoor
bloom or an excellent cut flower.

Versatility is one of the chrysan-themum's most outstanding characteristics. Mums provide a variety of colors, a vast range of plant sizes, a long flowering period, and are perhaps the world's most common cut flower after the rose.

Crocus tommasinianus, *one of the earliest crocuses to bloom, was named for de Tommasini, a nineteenth-century botanist from Trieste who studied this Yugoslavian native. The crocus has slender flowers that open in the sun to form a star shape.*

Large-flowered modern crocus hybrids are descendants of Crocus vernus, *whose purple or white flowers can be seen carpeting alpine meadows soon after the snow melts.*

The crocus is a true harbinger of spring, a welcome sight when trees are still bare, the wind still blows, and the winter cold hasn't yet given way to the warm days of spring.

Some crocuses, like Little Dorritt, are truly striped; others appear to have been washed in a contrasting color with a fine watercolor brush.

Crocuses are often grown where they can become naturalized, poking up between ground covers, carpeting trees and shrubs, or giving a golden gilt to the lawn.

Closely related to the daffodil, the jonquil, Narcissus jonquilla, has a fragrant flower similar to the daffodil's but differs from it in that its foliage is longer, narrower, and more rushlike.

Daffodil blossoms create a golden carpet in early spring. Hardy plants, daffodils will thrive as far north as southeastern Canada and the northern parts of the Plains states.

It is said that daffodils nod their heads in sorrow at Persephone's being kidnapped by Pluto. Nod they do, as they follow the sun from sunrise to sunset.

Iceland poppies provide contrasting color to the golden hues of daffodils in a midspring garden.

Convention implies that daffodils must be yellow, and, indeed, many are. But 100 years of breeding have introduced pink, orange, red, and white to these plants that dance in the spring sunshine.

Perhaps the most famous lines of poetry about the daffodil were written by William Wordsworth (1770–1850):

> I wandered lonely as a cloud
>   That floats on high o'er vales and hills,
> When all at once I saw a crowd,
>   A host, of golden daffodils.

DAHLIA

A New World native, the dahlia was discovered in the early sixteenth century by Spanish explorers of the Aztec empire. An easily grown garden flower, it became popular in Europe in the late 1700's and later returned to American gardens where its diverse flower forms, color, and natural ability to thrive are the reasons for the interest in this plant.

Growing wild in Mexico and Central America, the original dahlia of the Aztecs, *Dahlia imperialis,* was a tall (5 to 20 foot) plant with small, blood-red flowers. It is believed that it was used before the coming of the Spanish as a garden flower, a source of food, and for medicinal purposes. In 1519, the Cortez expedition discovered the dahlia, then called *cocoxochitl* (hollow-stem flower). This dahlia was collected and survived the journey across the Atlantic where it was first tended in Spanish monastery gardens.

Francisco Hernandez, physician to Philip II of Spain, wrote four books between 1570 and 1615 describing the plants and animals of Mexico. In addition to *cocoxochitl,* he also applied the names *acocotli* (water pipe) and *acocoxochitl* (water-pipe flower) to the dahlia because the Aztecs used the hollow stems to transport water. He noted many different flower forms, colors, and sizes than Cortez had found earlier.

An illustration of a dahlia appears in 1651 in the Italian work *Vitalis Mascardi,* which gives little information about it. Over a century later, Abbe Cavanilles of the Royal Botanical Gardens in Madrid sent seeds of the *cocoxochitl* to Andreas Dahl, who was a Swedish botanist and student of the botanical classifier Linnaeus. Dahl had dreams of using the plant's tubers as a new and useful vegetable similar to the potato, as they were used in Central and South America and Mexico, but he was disappointed to learn that the tubers were not to European tastes. Still, Dahl was intrigued with the plant and began selecting new varieties, crossing plant lines, and creating more diversified forms and colors. His work shed new light on the dahlia.

Following Dahl's work, the Spanish took a renewed interest in the plant and tried to reestablish their claim to the discovery. In 1789, the newly crowned King of Spain, Charles IV, held a festival to celebrate Spain's discovery of *cocoxochitl*. Because the Aztec name was difficult to translate, pronounce, and spell, Charles IV honored the Swedish botanist for his development of the new varieties and renamed the plant dahlia.

Dahlia plants were spread across Europe—first to France and then to the rest of western Europe and Russia. There they were named Georgina after a Russian horticulturist, Professor Georgi.

The English had received some plants from France, and dahlias were growing in the prestigious Kew Gardens in London by 1798. By the early 1800's, interest and breeding work in dahlias had intensified, and they were widely planted in European parks and other public places. In 1804, English nurseryman John Fraser published illustrations of the dahlia in Curtis's *Botanical Magazine,* and the plant's popularity grew even more.

No one could have foreseen the intense rivalry that would develop among European royalty for this flower. The dahlia became a treasured status symbol. It is said that Empress Josephine of France, famous, among other things, for her gardens at Malmaison, obtained dahlia seeds that had been stolen from the Spanish. She refused outright to share the plant with anyone. When a member of her court stole some of the tubers, from which both plants and seeds can be grown, the selfish Josephine became enraged and banned the innocent dahlia from her garden.

Botanical gardens, especially the one in Madrid, continued to collect dahlia seeds from the New World during the 1800's. Many were sent by Cervantes, who was keeper of the botanical garden in Mexico City. By the 1830's, the demand for the plants, seeds, and tubers soon outstripped the supply, causing prices to rise and fortunes to be lost. By 1836 an "Annual Dahlia Register" of hybrids had been published; it also carried dealers' advertisements.

It was not until later in the nineteenth century, when European demand was met, that the new dahlias arrived in the U.S., closer to their homeland. During the American Civil War, when supply lines with Europe were cut, New York City nurseryman Peter Henderson began producing his own dahlia seeds, tubers, and flowers. From that point on, dahlia breeding became popular in the U.S.

In 1872, a Dutch importer arranged for a shipment of dahlia tubers from Mexico. All died except one. From this one plant, which produced long, pointed red petals, new flower forms were developed. *D. juarezii* is said to have been named for the man who was President of Mexico from 1857 to 1872.

During this time, the dahlia found increasing favor; a British national newspaper offered a prize of £1,000 for the first "true blue" dahlia. The prize was never claimed, and could not be claimed today, because true blue in dahlias has still not been achieved. This did not dampen British spirit, however, for the National Dahlia Society was founded in England in 1881, and England still leads the world in the production of new varieties.

In the last 75 years, U.S. breeding and production of dahlias has been concentrated in the Santa Maria and Lompoc valleys in California, and one of the largest producers is located near Portland, Oregon. To recognize the popularity of this garden flower, the National Garden Bureau named 1988 the Year of the Dahlia. Breeding continues in England, Holland, and Japan.

At one time, if a gardener wanted a particular flower color, he had to buy tubers because plants grown from seeds did not grow true to color or form. Recent breeding achievements, such as the creation of the first F1 hybrid dahlias from seed, have changed that. There are now varieties called Sunny Red, Sunny Yellow, and Figaro White. Breeders look forward to the isolation and stabilization of more single colors in dahlias from seed, as well as to blue dahlias and fragrant dahlias.

Members of the Daisy Family, today's dahlias are hybrids. Most descend from *D. pinnata* (parent of the decorative types — dwarf dahlias and pompons) and were once called *D. variabilis,* and *D. coccinea* (parent of single-flowered hybrids). Some others are descended from *D. juarezii,* parent of the cactus-flowered forms. Available in all colors except blue and in a range of heights from low-growing border plants to giant specimens with dinner-plate-sized blooms, dahlias have a great number of flower forms. In order to describe the 3,000 or more named varieties of dahlia, the American Dahlia Society has established 12 classifications of flower form and size.

Single dahlias have daisylike blooms with a single ray of petals and may be solid colored or two toned. When a single flower has a ring of a contrasting color at the base of the petals, it is known as a *colarette.* In the anemone-flower form, there is one or more rows of petals, but the centers are tufted like pincushions. Dwarf, single-flowered dahlias are sometimes known as *mignons,* but this is not an "official" class of dahlia.

Fully double blooms whose long petals either curve inward toward the center, radiate straight from the center, or curve outward toward the base and grow on tall plants are known as cactus-flowered dahlias. Depending on the arrangement of the petals, they are called, respectively, incurved cactus, straight cactus, or semicactus. There are two types of decorative dahlias: the formal decorative has fully double flowers with broad petals that are regularly arranged; the informal decorative also has fully double flowers, but its petals are long, twisted, and irregularly arranged.

When blooms are large and ball shaped, the flowers are called ball dahlias. Flowers of the same shape but under two inches across are known as pompons. Peony dahlias have an open center and three to five rows of petals. Because some flowers defy the above descriptions, a twelfth, catch-all category known as miscellaneous was created.

Mexicans are proud of this flower — whose array of colors is similar to Mexican pottery and textiles — so much so that they have adopted the dahlia as their national floral emblem.

DAYLILY

The daylily, although it is lilylike in appearance, is not a true lily. But it is a close relative, a member of the same family. Daylilies belong to the genus *Hemerocallis,* which is derived from the Greek words for "beautiful for a day" because each flower lasts only one day. The blooms, however, are quickly replaced by others for a total blooming period of about six to eight weeks per plant. Although true lilies grow from bulbs, daylilies are perennials grown from tuberous roots.

Daylilies that are grown and cherished today for their ease of culture were originally grown thousands of years ago in the fields of central China. There they were planted not so much for their beauty as for their delicious and delicate flavor. The flower buds were eaten as a spring tonic, and leftovers were dried to be consumed during the winter. The Chinese not only liked the flavor of daylilies but also believed that they had the ability to relieve pain and cure kidney ailments.

In China, daylilies were originally known as *hsuan t'sao,* the plant of forgetfulness, because they caused a memory lapse and were used to lessen sorrow and relieve grief. They were also believed to have the power to effect the birth of a son if the mother wore flowers in "the girdle of her gown" during pregnancy. Leaves at that time were also used to treat burns and as forage for cattle.

Daylilies spread from China to Asia Minor, and the Greek herbalist and physician, Dioscorides, named the lemon daylily, *H. flava,* around the time of Christ. Daylilies later arrived in Europe thanks to the caravans that also brought Oriental silks. First popular in France, they quickly spread through Europe and were later brought to the U.S. by the religious refugee Huguenots, who took them to New York.

Daylilies were introduced into England by 1596, and it is believed that they were familiar to Shakespeare. Known as asphodel lilies, their roots looked like those of the asphodel, whereas their flowers resembled the lily's. Hostas, today sometimes called funkia or plantain lily, were once known as daylilies, but the name was dropped because of the confusion it caused.

Daylilies, summer-blooming mainstays of the perennial garden, bloom chiefly in shades of yellow, orange, apricot, red, pink, and violet. There are still no pure whites or true blues. Those of yellow color usually carry the perfume of the sweetly scented *H. lilioasphodelus,* once known as *H. flava,* the lemon daylily. This plant, although a native from Siberia to Japan, has been growing wild in pasture lands in Europe for so long that it was once thought to be native to the foothills of the Alps. Common in European cottage gardens during the mid-seventeenth century, the daylily reached America by the 1800's.

Daylilies with orange flowers can usually be traced back to the scentless *H. fulva*, or tawny daylily, which was well known in Europe by the sixteenth century. It has become a wildflower in the eastern U.S., a remarkable feat for it does not set seeds. The thousands of existing roadside plants got there by spreading their roots. A naturally occurring pink form of this plant is the parent of all pink- and red-flowered modern hybrids.

Nothing more happened with daylilies in the western world until the mid-nineteenth century. A double form of *H. fulva* was brought from Japan in 1860, where it had been known for about 150 years, and it immediately began to be propagated and sold in London. A variegated form with double flowers arrived four years later and was known as a Kwanso type. In 1897, flowers with deeply colored patches on the petals were made available.

New varieties arrived in Europe regularly from Japan, whereas others were sent directly to North America and forwarded across the Atlantic. Americans took a great shine to daylilies, and today both amateur and professional breeders from North America produce many of the best varieties.

One attraction of the daylily is the ease with which new hybrids are produced. As many as 900 new cultivars are registered with the American Hemerocallis Society each year, and to date the total number of varieties goes beyond a staggering 45,000. Many have been lost to horticultural history.

Daylily flowers can vary from less than three inches to more than six inches across. Rock gardeners prefer the dwarf plants, whereas others choose types that stretch as high as eight feet. Some are single, others double; many have decorative and ruffled petal edges. Most daylilies open in the morning and close by dusk, but some open in late afternoon and close the following morning. Breeders have been trying to manipulate the daylily's routine, but so far the longest any flower has remained open is 16 hours.

Daylilies are still used in food preparation today. Their blossoms are delicious stuffed with salads or stir fried, and their buds are often used in soups (they're great in hot and sour soup), stews, and pasta dishes. Peeled and sliced, pieces of the tubers are delicious in salads.

DELPHINIUM

Sometimes called the queen of garden plants, the delphinium is the high point of a perennial garden, literally and figuratively. Bearing very large and beautiful spikes of flowers in shades of blue, purple, lavender, pink, yellow, and white, the delphinium grows quite tall.

The shape of the flower suggested both the common and botanical names for the delphinium. The Greek word *delphinion* means "larkspur," and is a diminutive of the word *delphin,* which means "dolphin." The long spur of the flower reminded some people of the nose of a dolphin. The spur also suggested names such as larkspur and lark's claw. Shakespeare referred to it as lark's heel.

The annual larkspur was for many years included in the *Delphinium* genus, although it now has its own genus, *Consolida.* Legend states that the larkspur originated during the ancient battle at Troy, where the warrior Achilles was slain. His mother asked that her son's armor be given to the most heroic Greek warrior. The brave Ajax expected to be chosen, but Ulysses was picked instead, and Ajax, depressed over the turn of events, committed suicide. Where his blood spilled is where the small blue larkspur first grew. The plant was called *D. acajis* after Ajax, although this story is also often associated with the hyacinth.

The delphinium is native across the Northern Hemisphere through China, Siberia, Europe, and North America. The perennial delphinium of today's garden evolved from the annual larkspur. The earliest perennial species, *D. staphisagria,* was grown in gardens during the fifteenth century. It reached its height of popularity in the eighteenth century and had short but attractive spikes of purplish blue flowers, however, it was grown more for its insect-repelling abilities than its ornamental value. It is now very rare.

Concurrently, the annual larkspur in both single-stem and branched-stem forms was being improved. By the end of the sixteenth century, red, pink, and white forms had been added to the naturally occurring blues. Double flowers were created and became popular by the seventeenth and eighteenth centuries. Many of the nineteenth-century varieties are still grown today.

Candle larkspur, *D. elatum,* is typical of the perennial delphinium, with flowers growing in dense spikes up to six feet tall. Native to the central regions of Europe and Russia, it was growing in gardens by the late sixteenth century. Double forms were grown by the seventeenth century. Originally, it grew to be only four feet tall; but once it was crossbred with *D. grandiflorum,* also known as Chinese or Siberian delphinium, in the early 1800's, the taller forms were achieved.

Candle larkspur is the parent of many of today's hybrids, which are sometimes called Elatum hybrids. Florists and nurserymen crossbred throughout the 1800's, and by the end of the century had produced large numbers of beautiful hybrids. There were a few double-flowered varieties on the market, with flowers of yellow, cream, and white appearing first. These new colors were achieved by introducing the red-flowered California natives *D. cardinale* and *D. nudicaule* and the yellow-flowered Persian native *D. semibarbatum* into the breeding lines. By the early 1900's, delphiniums could be counted on to be more reliably hardy.

One of the best known of the hybrid groups is the Belladonna hybrids, *D. X belladonna,* which have 3- to 5-foot stalks bearing multiple spikes of white or blue flowers. They appeared in the late 1800's and were first used by florists as a cut flower. The double-flowered forms appeared in the 1880's and were prized by florists because the blooms were sterile, which means they are able to last longer in flower arrangements.

The now-popular Pacific Coast hybrids first appeared in the 1950's. They were bred by Frank Reinelt in California, and at first had names relating to King Arthur and the Knights of the Round Table. The flowers are mostly double, in shades of white, pink, lavender, pale or dark blue, violet, and purple, and most of the flowers have a central cluster of short petals known as a bee. It was not until 1960, however, that the first perennial delphinium with pink flowers was created.

Shorter delphiniums, which are often treated as annuals, have recently been developed. These include the Dwarf Pacific delphiniums and the Connecticut Yankees, which reach heights of only two to two and one half feet.

For years, delphiniums have been used as a strong external medicine. In ancient times, it was believed that if scorpions and other beasts ingested the seeds and leaves, they would become powerless. Seeds were at one time ground into powder and used for toothaches. Water distilled from the flowers was used to strengthen the eyes, and writers of old believed that merely to look at the flowers would have the same effect. Some species were used to destroy head lice; records show it was used for this purpose by the armies at the Battle of Waterloo and during the American Civil War. Armies also used delphinium plants to dress wounds. However, some of the wild species are highly poisonous if ingested and have been known to cause the death of grazing cattle.

Delphiniums are not the easiest plants to grow, as they require full sun, cool temperatures, light, fertile soil, and staking. The plants are so spectacular, however, that the rewards are well worth the efforts that gardeners must make to grow them.

DOGWOOD

Except for a single Peruvian/Chilean species, all dogwoods are native to the Northern Hemisphere. As shrubs or small trees, they are true four-star plants, renowned for their beautiful flowers, colorful berries, attractive form, and foliage.

Dogwoods are ancient plants and are mentioned in the writings of Virgil, Homer, and Theophrastus. The genus name, *Cornus,* comes from the Latin word for horn, because the wood of *C. mas,* one of the first known dogwoods, resembles the polished horns of an ox. The common name is a corruption of the old word dagwood (or daggerwood), because daggers for skewering meat were made from the older species. The name has since been transferred to the entire genus.

Most of the North American species are native east of the Rockies; and the most spectacular of these is *C. florida,* the flowering dogwood, which has flowers of white or pink. Its flat-topped crown of spreading horizontal branches lends a layered Oriental look to its winter silhouette. Flowering dogwoods are among the easiest of trees to identify even when they are not in bloom, as the flower buds are onion shaped and the leaf veins curve around and follow the edge of the leaf margin.

Flowering dogwood is very similar in appearance to its western counterpart, *C. nuttalli,* the western or mountain dogwood. Although it will only grow well in the cool, moist climate of the Pacific Northwest, it is one of the only dogwoods that bloom in spring and again in fall. The creek dogwood, *C. X californica,* also exhibits that same characteristic.

The red-branched *C. sanguinea,* is common in England in hedges and thickets and is known by a number of names such as European dogwood, prickwood, pegwood, blood-twig dogwood, skewerwood, or dogberry. The white wood is very hard and, like that of various other dogwoods, is used for making ladders, wheels, skewers, wooden spoons, and other implements.

One of the brightest red-branched dogwoods is *C. alba,* whose species name refers to its white flowers and bluish-white fruits. It was first discovered in 1741 and is called Tatarian dogwood because it is native to Siberia, where the Tatar people of Turkish descent reside. The Siberian dogwood, which will survive the coldest of winters, is a variety of *C. alba.*

Red osier dogwood, *C. sericea,* is the North American counterpart to *C. alba.* It also has red branches that are outstanding when seen against a backdrop of winter snow. Its common name refers to the pliability of its branches; osiers are willows used to make baskets and woven furniture. In cultivation since 1656, osier dogwood has bark that was once smoked by the Indians. A variety of this species, *flaviramea,* has golden yellow twigs and naturally is called golden-twig dogwood.

Two ground-hugging species of dogwood are bunchberry or creeping dogwood, *C. canadensis,* and Lapland cornel, *C. suecia.* They are native around the world north of the Arctic circle. Bunchberry is often called puddingberry because it was put to that use by the Indians and the early American settlers. The bright red berries of the Lapland cornel are eaten by the Eskimos.

Cornelian cherry, *C. mas,* is unique among dogwoods. It is a spreading tree with clouds of small yellow flowers that bloom in early spring before the leaves open. Its shiny red cherrylike fruit, which blooms in fall, is used in preserves and jellies .

C. kousa, Japanese or Kousa dogwood, is one of the latest dogwoods to bloom in spring and has white to pinkish flowers with pointed rather than rounded petals. If the birds don't get to it first, the fruit, which looks like raspberries, is a spectacular sight in autumn. The peeling bark of this tree is also very beautiful. *C. kousa chinensis,* the most recent dogwood to be known, was found by plant explorers at the edge of the Himalayas in northern Assam in 1950.

Most dogwoods have leaves that are opposite each other on the stems. There are exceptions to this, as seen in the pagoda dogwood, *C. alternifolia.* It's not as showy as its cousins, but it survives harsher winters and has tiers of slightly fragrant white flowers in late spring and blue-black fruit borne on red stems in the fall.

Many dogwood blossoms are actually clusters of tiny flowers surrounded by large, showy, colored bracts, although most of the shrubby species lack these bracts. The shrubby species have their own merits, however; in addition to the colorful bark many of them exhibit, they are tougher, more resilient plants. Together, the tree and shrub species of dogwoods form the backbone of the woody plant garden.

FUCHSIA

Once upon a time, high in the mountains of Chile, a British sailor found a fuchsia plant and took it back to England to his wife. The plant produced beautiful nodding flowers never before seen in England and created an immediate sensation. James Lee, a prominent nurseryman from Hammersmith, saw the plant growing in the lady's window box and convinced the sailor's wife to sell it to him. Through Lee's efforts, the popularity of breeding and growing fuchsia continues today.

Even though the fuchsia did not become vogue until the end of the eighteenth century when James Lee started propagating and selling it, it was known by at least the fourteenth century, when the Incas in Peru were growing *Fuchsia boliviana* for its edible berries. In about 1700, French monk and botanist Father Jean Carole Plumier, found *F. triphylla,* a shrubby plant with scarlet flowers. His discovery was made accidentally on the island of Hispaniola in the Caribbean while he was searching for the cinchona tree, from which quinine is extracted. He named the plant for Leonard Fuchs, a sixteenth-century botanist and professor of medicine, but unfortunately the plant was then lost for over 100 years.

During the eighteenth century, several species of fuchsia made their way to Europe from Mexico and South America. These included *F. arborescens,* a Mexican plant with reddish purple and lilac flowers that could reach 25 feet in height, and *F. coccinea,* a shrubby plant from Brazil with red and violet flowers. By the end of the century, *F. lycioides,* with its small pink flowers, was growing in England, and crosses were being made.

Breeding with fuchsias became very popular in the early nineteenth century. Until 1840, the only flower colors being produced were red and blue or red and purple, but during that year, the first two-tone with white fuchsia was created. In 1848, the first striped variety was hybridized, a pink and blue, and in 1850, the first double flowers appeared. Across Europe, especially in France, Belgium, and England, hundreds of new varieties began to appear. One of the most prominent hybridizers of the time was James Lye, who worked between 1860 and 1889.

The Victorian era was the heyday for the fuchsia. By the end of World War I, fuchias began to decline in popularity, and only a few private collections were left. Across the Atlantic, however, interest in breeding fuchsias had begun in California. The American Fuchsia Society was founded in 1929 and the following year three of its officers went to England to collect varieties from which they could start a breeding program. Four dozen varieties were taken to California and were the basis of the vast numbers of fuchsias that followed.

Forgetting their disfavor with anything Victorian, the English once again took interest in the fuchsia and formed the Fuchsia Society in 1938. By 1936, when the first "Check List of Fuchsias" was published, there were 2,000 known varieties. The most recent issue of the same publication contains almost 10,000 known varieties.

F. magellanica, a Chilean species with red and purple flowers, and *F. fulgens,* a two-toned red species from Mexico, are the primary parents of many of our modern hybrids known today as *F. X hybrida,* the familiar, usually two-toned flowers of red, purple, white, and pink grown in American gardens in hanging baskets. Although most of these hybrid fuchsias will not survive if subjected to frost, there are other species in England, Wales, and Scotland where hedges of fuchsias often 20 feet high attract tourists to the countryside in late summer and fall.

Interest in fuchsias is extremely high in the Pacific Northwest, where the climate is so favorable. Because the fuchsia is native to high mountain slopes from Mexico to South America, it grows best in gardens where the same climatic conditions can be met — moderate warmth, moist soil, humidity, and shade.

Because of the shape of the flowers, fuchsias are often known as lady's eardrops, although some regard the flower as looking more like a hoop skirt. The color fuchsia stems from the reddish purple tones present on so many of the species and varieties.

GERANIUMS

Geraniums are the second most popular flowering annual in North America, falling between the leading impatiens and the third-place flower, the petunia.

Garden geraniums, members of the genus *Pelargonium,* were first brought to Europe from South Africa in 1631 on a Dutch trading ship. Once the Dutch East India Company established its colony in Cape Town in 1652, more plants of this South African native began appearing in Holland and England. The first species was *P. triste,* the "sad" geranium, a bit of a misnomer for it had delicate sprays of yellow and brown flowers and a powerfully sweet scent at night. It remained popular through the seventeenth and eighteenth centuries and was the basis of a group of nineteenth-century hybrids that are now extinct.

A trickle of other species came to Europe during the seventeenth and eighteenth centuries, and by the nineteenth century Europe was flooded with new geraniums. The geranium of today, *P. X hortorum,* is a complex hybrid of *P. zonale,* introduced in 1710, *P. inquinans,* introduced in 1714, and other species. Geraniums with variegated leaves were known by 1724, and leaves with white margins were around by 1785. By the mid-1800's, many geraniums were grown just for the beauty of their leaves — many gardeners removed the brightly colored flowers.

John Bartram, a Philadelphia botanist, received the first geranium seeds in the colonies in 1760, and the flowers soon became popularly regarded as synonymous with home and hospitality. Early records show that Thomas Jefferson collected geraniums during a trip to France. Settlers carried them across the country with their household goods as the wagon trains headed West.

Garden geraniums, which are sometimes called zonal geraniums because of a dark-colored band that appears on some of the leaves, were single flowered until 1864, when the first double-flowered form was introduced by Lemoine in France. The first white flowers had been discovered in 1850, and today geraniums may be white, pink, rose, red, salmon, coral, violet, or orange.

Geraniums reached a height of popularity during Victorian times, but it was not until the mid-twentieth century that they were able to grow true to color from seed; until that time, geraniums were bred from cuttings to maintain varieties and color. In 1963, the first hybrid geranium from seed was created at the Pennsylvania State University and was appropriately called Nittany Lion. It was followed in 1968 by the Carefree series. Sprinter Scarlet, the first early blooming geranium variety, made its breakthrough in 1973.

After the introduction of Sprinters, the Sooners, Flash, Smash Hit, Firecracker, Ringo, Mustang, and Orbit varieties became available. University research aided the commercial plant growers with the discovery of growth regulators that would keep plants more compact, an increased understanding of supplemental lighting in greenhouses, and a method to keep flowers from shattering and falling off the plants during the transition from greenhouse to garden.

The even newer Hollywood, Diamond, and Pinto geraniums took the geranium to the forefront of early blooming, compactness, and heavy flowering. Steady Red was the first double-flowered form from seed; it was introduced in 1985. There are still, of course, many geraniums that continue to be propagated from cuttings. Their culture has given the greenhouse industry insight into the importance of propagation of disease-free stock, a process known as virus-indexing, and of growing under sanitary conditions.

Cousin to the garden geranium is the ivy geranium, *P. peltatum,* which first came to Holland in 1700. Popular for its cascading habit in hanging baskets and its ivy-shaped leaves, ivy geraniums still represent almost 50 percent of all geraniums grown in Europe, especially northern Europe, where they thrive in the cool climate and dominate window boxes. In 1986, Summer Showers, the first ivy geranium grown from seed, was introduced.

Trailing geraniums have loose clusters of small flowers; however, crosses between ivy geraniums and zonal geraniums have the best of both: a cascading habit, and large flowers and heat resistance. The first cross between garden geraniums and ivy geraniums that could be grown from seeds is Red Fountain, which was introduced in 1983.

Some confusion appears in the geranium clan because of the large number of perennial species in a genus known as *Geranium.* Although the plants are related, they are distinctly different, the perennials being small-flowered, primarily ground-hugging plants. However, the many scented-leaf geraniums are in the *Pelargonium* species, and although their flowers are not showy, their leaves carry a variety of delicious fragrances.

Scented geraniums that had not been known before became very popular in Victorian gardens. Gardeners of the day often planted scented geraniums where long and full clothing would brush against the leaves, releasing the flower's fragrance into the air. Potpourris, sachets, finger bowls, and even jellies soon captured the aroma of such geraniums as *P. capitatum* or *P. graveolens,* often used to replace the more expensive attar of roses in perfumes; *P. crispum,* with a lemon scent; *P. tomentosum,* with peppermint aroma; *P. clorinda,* with the fragrance of eucalyptus; *P. quercifolium,* the oak-leaf geranium, with a spicy scent something like incense; and *P. fragrans,* which is reminiscent of nutmeg. *P. odoratissimum* has been used to flavor apple jelly, whereas *P. asperum* can be used as a substitute for sage. The Turkish and the French have been growing scented geraniums since the mid-nineteenth century to use the leaves in less expensive perfumes.

The last major class of geraniums is the Martha Washingtons, *P. X domesticum,* which are complex hybrids developed in the late 1800's. More popular in the past than they are today, Martha Washingtons, also known as regals, may be on the rise again; plant breeders are experimenting to improve this fancy-flowered geranium and develop one that is not daunted by high summer temperatures.

Geraniums are sometimes referred to as crane's bills, because the seed pods are long and pointed like a crane's beak. The word geranium comes from the Greek *geranos,* which means crane.

Since breeding began several hundred years ago, over 10,000 different geranium cultivars have been developed. It is not surprising that this plant continues to hold onto its No. 2 rank among garden flowers.

IMPATIENS

The ultimate success story in the plant world is about the new kid on the flower block—the impatiens. Thirty-five years ago, it was in limited use as a garden annual. Today, it is North America's most popular annual flower, because breeders have made it so much better and because it is one of the easiest plants to grow. It thrives in both shade and sun, and is not bothered a bit by heat and humidity. Flowers dominate these plants in all colors except true yellow.

The impatiens was introduced to Europe from Zanzibar, an island off the coast of East Africa, in 1896. Although known today as *Impatiens wallerana,* it was then called *I. sultanii* for the Sultan of the Arabic island, and also developed the common name sultana. The impatiens also found its way to the New World from Africa on early slave and trading ships and quickly became naturalized.

Impatiens became popular in Europe as a potted plant, but it was tall-growing and often lanky. With the introduction of a new variety of impatiens called Babies in the mid-1960's, a breakthrough was on the horizon. The dwarf habit of the Babies brought them into use in the garden and inspired breeders to delve into cross breeding with this plant.

By 1969, the first hybrid impatiens, the Pixies from Pan American Seed Company and the Shadeglows from Harris Seed Company, were on the market. An increase in the popularity of shade gardening led to the development of the Elfins by Pan American Seed Company in the early 1970's. These new plants were smaller and more free flowering than ever before. Impatiens sales soared, coinciding with the U.S. oil crisis and a rise in all types of gardening.

In 1981, All-America Selections gave its highest award for a new flower to a variety of impatiens called Blitz. This was the first (but not the last) time since its founding in 1933 that it had awarded this distinction to an impatiens, a fact which further explains the relative "newness" of this garden flower.

Thanks to the dedication of a man named Claude Hope, impatiens are what they are today. From his breeding facilities at Linda Vista, Costa Rica, Hope has been responsible for many of the improvements of impatiens, including the Super Elfins. He is also responsible for creating Duet and Rosette, the first double-flowered impatiens that can be grown from seed, a breeding feat that took him 15 years to accomplish.

Hybrid impatiens flowers must be hand-pollinated in a greenhouse to produce seeds, a time-consuming and labor-intensive chore. Seed companies have chosen the highlands in Central America, chiefly Costa Rica and Guatemala, and Kenya in East Africa, as the primary sites for this work because the light intensity is high, the temperature is moderate year round, there is a good supply of water, and there is inexpensive labor available.

The impatiens got its name from the way the seed pods coil at maturity, which causes the release of the seed in a most impatient manner. It is sometimes called snapweed. Busy Lizzie and patient Lucy are two other names associated with the impatiens.

In 1968, a team of plant explorers and botanists discovered a new impatiens, the New Guinea impatiens, named for the island on which it was found. Although this plant blooms, its flowers are more sparse than those of garden impatiens. Its crowning glory is its foliage, which is brightly striped, marked, or blotched in bright green, yellow, red, or maroon. Claude Hope has bred many new New Guinea impatiens from the original stock.

A close relative of the impatiens is the garden balsam, *I. balsamina,* a native of tropical India, China, and the Malay Peninsula that was known in Europe by the end of the fifteenth century. It is often called touch-me-not because of the characteristic of the seed capsule to release its seeds at the slightest touch, and was a favorite in Victorian gardens for its large, waxy flowers in tones of red, pink, orange, yellow, and purple.

Another relative is jewelweed, *I. capensis,* one of the few members of the genus native to the Americas. It was used by Native Americans to treat skin disorders and is still used today to relieve the itch caused by poison ivy.

In less than 35 years, the impatiens has gone from virtual obscurity to being the most popular flowering annual. There are few other flowers that can match such a quick rise to fame.

IRIS

The iris is a unique flower, with three upright petals called standards and three drooping petals called falls. Many have a fuzzy stripe on the petals and are known as bearded irises. They bloom in nearly every color and have flat, pointed, swordlike leaves. When the flowers do not have beards, the petals are more horizontal and the leaves are narrow and reedlike. The three largest petals of the iris have long represented faith, wisdom, and valor.

Irises are divided into two categories: those that grow from rhizomes and those that grow from bulbs. The rhizomatous groups include the common bearded irises (*Iris. X germanica*), the Siberian iris (*I. sibirica*) and the Japanese iris (*I. kaempferi*). The common bearded iris, sometimes called German iris, has been in cultivation the longest; it is so ancient that its origins are unknown, but it has been growing in the wild across Europe and Asia for thousands of years. The Siberian iris, with its graceful lavender, purple, or blue flowers, hailed from central and eastern Europe and Russia and was a popular garden plant by the sixteenth century. The Japanese iris, which is beardless, was introduced from the country for which it is named in 1857.

Spring flower arrangements commonly contain *I. xiphium,* or Dutch iris, a bulbous plant with white, yellow, purple, or blue flowers. Its origins are actually in Spain and Portugal, and it has been a florists' flower since the 1700's. Early blooming rock gardens are frequent homes for two other iris bulbs: *I. danfordiae,* with its tiny yellow flowers, first discovered in Turkey in 1884; and *I. reticulata,* a miniature iris with blue or purple blooms that was introduced into Europe from the Caucasus in 1808.

The iris was named for the Greek goddess of the rainbow because of its many colorful flowers. Iris was the word used to describe the "eye of heaven" in ancient times. It was believed that the goddess Iris took messages of love from the eye of heaven to earth, using the rainbow as a bridge. Because of this, the flower became a symbol of communication. Iris was also the name given to the colored portion of the eye, and many believe that each of us carries a piece of heaven with us in our eyes.

Greek men would often plant iris on the graves of their lovers in tribute to the goddess Iris, whose duty it was to carry the lost souls to everlasting happiness. Ancient Greeks also used the iris in perfumes. The Romans, Egyptians, and Moors grew the iris for its medicinal value, using it to treat epilepsy, fever, chills, headaches, and snake bites. Irises have been included in herb gardens since the Middle Ages. Its roots were mixed with honey and wine and used for colds, coughs, and stomachaches.

In Germany, the iris root was put into barrels of beer to keep the brew from getting stale. In France, it was used to improve the bouquet of wines. In Russia, it was used with honey and ginger in a drink. In England, it was added to wash water to sweetly scent the clothes. In the Mediterranean, plants of *Iris albicans* are used to bind sandy soil against erosion. In the seventeenth century, followers of Mohammed planted *I. X germanica,* the most common bearded iris on graves, thereby spreading plants across northern Africa and into Europe.

The story goes that at one time in Japan, people were not allowed to grow any flowers in their gardens that were not approved by the Emperor. The iris was not among the prohibited flowers, so the Japanese grew them on their rooftops and the name for *Iris tectorum,* Japanese rooftop iris, sticks today.

A variety of iris, *I. X germanica,* is the major source of orris, which is made from the dried and powdered rhizome. Sweetly scented like a violet, it is used in perfumery, and is also used as a fixative in sachets and potpourris because it enhances other aromas. In medieval times, it was used to take the musty smell out of clothes and to powder the hair. Mexico exports tons of the root to France each year for use in perfumes and cosmetics. Flowers of the yellow flag iris, *I. pseudacorus,* are used to make yellow dyes, whereas the roots are used for brown and black dyes. Blue-violet dyes are made from purple-flowered irises.

In the year 496, King Clovis I of France was trapped during battle between an enemy army and a broad river. Seeing a yellow flag iris growing in the middle of the river, he knew it was shallow enough to cross, and he marched his army across to victory. Taking the incident as a sign from God, he and many of his followers converted to Christianity on Christmas Day, adopting the iris as their floral symbol. It is believed that Charles IV, who reigned in France from 1294 to 1328, was the first king to place the iris on the French flag, although Louis VII had used it on his banner during the Crusades a century earlier and named it "flower of Louis." Today it is still known as the fleur-de-lis and is the floral symbol of France.

The history of the hybridizing of irises is sketchy prior to the early 1800's. Pioneer work was done in England and France, with the U.S. joining in the early twentieth century. The American Iris Society and the British Iris Society were founded in 1920 and 1922 respectively and, with the increase and improvement of communications, transportation, and world travel, irises are now known and appreciated all over the world.

Although the dahlia was discovered by botanists who traveled with the conquistadores in Central America in the sixteenth century, it did not receive its modern name until the eighteenth century, when it was first brought to Europe.

The dahlia was named for Dr.
Andreas Dahl, a relatively unknown
Swedish botanist whose mentor,
Abbé Cavanilles, curator of the
Royal Botanic Gardens in Madrid,
uncharacteristically allowed the
plant to be named for his assistant.

Dahlia flowers come in many different shapes. These dahlias, known as decoratives, are the most widely grown of the modern varieties that beautify gardens and brighten indoor arrangements.

Single-flowered dahlias, such as Coltness Mix, fill garden beds with low-growing plants and a riot of color — all from one packet of seed.

Lavender dahlias are favorites with everyone, perhaps because their color is the closest thing to blue, a color that is yet to be achieved with dahlias.

The first cactus-flowered dahlia, Dahlia juarezii, *was created in Holland in 1872, and from it sprung every modern variety of cactus-flowered dahlia grown today.*

One of the most endearing characteristics of the dahlia is the ease with which it combines two, three, and sometimes even more colors in one flower. These combinations are known as variegates, suffusions, or blends.

Deriving their name from the Greek for "beautiful for a day," Hemerocallis, *or daylilies, have flowers that last only one day. Fortunately, they are quickly replaced by buds that have been waiting their turn to bloom.*

The daylily is possibly the most responsive perennial on earth. With minimum care plants will double or triple in size in no time, displaying a sort of gratitude for their planting by producing more and more flowers each year.

Hemerocallis fulva *was first described in Europe in 1576 and is now the most widely distributed daylily worldwide and the most common daylily growing wild in fields across North America.*

The delphinium has long been dubbed the "Queen of the Perennial Garden Plants"; its culture and care is a challenge, but no gardener worth his loam would not grow it.

There is little more beautiful or rewarding than the sight of the six- to eight-foot spike of a mature delphinium, which seems well worth any trouble or expense in growing these magnificent flowers.

Delphinium elatum, *candle larkspur, has been cultivated since 1578 and is the basis for many of today's modern hybrids.*

Tall, bold spikes of delphinium exhibit blooms of purple and lavender, common delphinium colors.

Today's perennial delphinium descended from the annual larkspur, which has now been moved into its own genus and species, Consolida ambiqua.

Some delphinium flowers have a white or black central portion which is known as a bee. This characteristic is useful in identifying the different varieties.

In winter, when the snow is thick and the soul yearns for signs of life, the mottled bark and intricate branches of the dogwood glisten promisingly in the welcome sunshine.

A sure sign that spring has come to stay is the appearance of the four-petalled blooms of dogwood that grace front lawns, public parks, wooded hillsides, and luscious meadows.

Gracefully drooping, the leaves of dogwood reflect the summer sun as the red berries begin to form.

Autumn frosts bring blazing scarlet leaves to the dogwood. A closer inspection will reveal that next year's flower buds have already appeared.

53

Flowering dogwood, Cornus florida, *is but one of a number of members of this genus, which contains many other trees and shrubs, all unique in their own right.*

The closest relative of flowering dogwood is C. florida rubra. *Other relatives are Cornelian cherry, Kousa dogwood, red-osier dogwood, and yellow-twigged dogwood.*

Dogwoods are sometimes called cornels, a derivative of their Latin name. The name dogwood is a corruption of dagwood or dagger-wood, since daggers for skewering meat were once made from the wood.

Fuchsias are sometimes known as lady's eardrops, because they resemble earrings. Some also think they look like old-fashioned hoop skirts.

Not all fuchsias have the well-known, full flowers with flaring petals; Firecracker has long, slender flowers.

Before 1840, all fuchsias were either red and purple or red and blue. Since then, the color range has expanded into white, cream, pink, and orange.

57

Although all of the common garden geraniums, Pelargonium X hortorum, *are known as zonal geraniums, not all display the dark zoning on the leaves seen here.*

Geraniums are second in popularity among flowering annuals. Red geraniums were at one time the most popular, but are now giving way to pinks, corals, salmons, and other lighter colors.

Water lily ponds are dramatically edged with massed beds of common garden geraniums.

At one time, all geraniums were grown from cuttings. But since 1963, as a result of work done at the University of Pennsylvania, they have been grown from seeds as well.

Scented geraniums are usually not grown for their flowers, but for their foliage, which may carry aromas of rose, orange, lemon, line, pine, nutmeg, turpentine, apple, almond, and peppermint.

The fancy flowers of the Martha Washington, or regal, geranium are popular in the cool climates of the Pacific Northwest, where these plants flourish.

Not all geraniums have the characteristic rounded flowerhead of the common garden geranium. There are almost 300 other species of geraniums, many rare, with unique, usually five-petaled flowers.

Impatiens are North America's most popular annual flower, having shown an amazing surge in garden use; as recently as the mid-1960's, very few impatiens were used in the garden.

Preceding pages: *A mixed border of perennials and annuals paint a colorful portrait of flowers.*

While many impatiens are solid colored, others show a unique starred pattern on their flowers.

Accent Lilac is one of a series of
new, dwarf impatiens with varieties
of white, apricot, pink, rose,
scarlet, orange, violet, coral, red,
and salmon flowers.

The Siberian iris, Iris sibirica, has gracefully pendant petals known as falls. It is actually native to central Europe and Russia and is only rarely found in Siberia, but it is the hardiest iris.

The flowers of the common bearded iris, Iris X germanica, can be solid colored, two-toned (as pictured here), or a blend of three or more colors.

According to myth, the iris was made for the Greek goddess of the rainbow, also named Iris, and displayed many colors. Irises are known as flags for the same reason, and because of the way they furl in the early summer breezes.

Velvety irises stand bold in front of a mixed garden.

The Douglas iris, Iris douglasiana,
*grows wild on bare headlands and
grassy coastal hills from Santa
Barbara, California, north to
southern Oregon.*

The iris is the floral symbol of France and has been since the fifth century. King Louis VII named it the "flower of Louis" in the thirteenth century and it is still known today as the fleur-de-lis.

The tall bearded iris Immortality reblooms in a northeast garden. Most irises will usually only rebloom in warm climates such as California.

LILY

The lily is one of the world's oldest plants. Cultivated by the ancient Sumerians in the Tigris and Euphrates Valley, these bulbs have been grown for at least 5,000 years in the area that is now Iraq. There was even a Sumerian city named Susa, which means lily. No one knows for sure if the flower was named for the city, or the city named for the flower.

Greek and Roman mythologies mention the lily often, as do the legends of China and Japan. Lilies have grown wild in these and other parts of the Northern Hemisphere since ancient times.

The Romans associated the lily with Juno, the queen of the heavens, the goddess of marriage, and wife of Jupiter. According to the myth, when Juno was nursing her foster son Hercules, excess milk fell from her breast. Part of it stayed in the heavens and became the Milky Way; the rest fell to earth, and white lilies sprang up from where it landed.

Lilies have long been connected with religion. They were thought to be sacred to the Minoan goddess Britomartis, were considered the flower of St. Anthony, the protector of marriages, were considered a symbol of the Virgin Mary, and were a symbol for Venus, the Roman goddess of love. The flower most often associated with Easter is *L. longiflorum eximium,* the Easter Lily, and on July 2, the day when Christians celebrate the Visitation of the Blessed Virgin, lilies are used to decorate churches.

White lilies have always been used as a symbol of peace, good, and beauty. The lily is thought to be the sacred flower of motherhood, able to predict the birth of a male child. Superstitious Europeans once believed it protected them from ghosts and witchcraft.

Lilies have been used medicinally and cosmetically for centuries. The Romans used them to treat corns and sores on the feet, and the Greeks also made them into salves and ointments. Lilies, mixed with yarrow and boiled in oil, were used for burns, and lily seeds mixed with water were ingested for snakebite. White lilies were thought to cure the bite of a rabid dog. Lily bulbs ground with honey were used on the face to clear the complexion and make wrinkles disappear. Washing hair with lilies, ashes, and lye was done to bleach it to blonde.

Lilies have always been associated with majesty, royalty, and war. The Moors adopted it as their symbol in the eighth century and took plants across Africa and into Spain and Portugal as they conquered. The House of Orange in Holland used the orange lily as its political symbol. Lilies appear in the coats-of-arms of many colleges and universities, especially in Europe.

Depending on the species, lilies can be selected to provide bloom from late spring through early fall. One of the first to bloom is Turk's-cap lily, *Lilium martagon,* which has drooping, reflexed petals and grows wild from Portugal to Mongolia. Purple varieties of this lily were known by the sixteenth century, and double forms were known in the eighteenth and nineteenth centuries, although they are now rare or extinct.

Next in the bloom sequence is *L. candidum* and the Candidum hybrids, also known as Madonna lilies, which have fragrant, pure white flowers. This lily, native to the Near East, was known in Europe by at least the tenth century. It was very popular in the sixteenth-century garden and a frequent accompaniment to portraits of the saints, although it was not named until the end of the nineteenth century. It has long been regarded as a symbol of purity and innocence, and it reigned alone in popularity in Europe until the sixteenth century, reaching America by the seventeenth century.

Native to North America, the American hybrids have nodding, spotted flowers of pink, red, orange, and yellow. The native North American lilies first traveled to Europe in the seventeenth century; as settlers moved West, they discovered more and more new species on the Pacific coast, and reintroduced them to Europe. One of the most famous American hybrid strains, the Bellinghams, was started in California in 1918. Oregon Bulb Farms is one of the world's largest lily hybridizers and producers, and it was the founder, Mr. Jan de Graaff, who in 1947 created the orange variety Enchantment, for years the standardbearer for the industry.

The American hybrids bloom at about the same time as the freckle-faced Asiatic hybrids, including the well-known Mid-Century hybrids that first appeared in the mid-nineteenth century (Mr. de

Graaff, a century later, created another series of Mid-Century hybrids). Following on their heels in bloom are the flouncy-petaled Aurelian hybrids, which bloom in many colors, some with yellow throats or maroon stripes. They were first created between 1928 and 1938. The real beginning of lily breeding started when lilies from Japan were crossbred in Europe and the first Asiatic hybrids were created.

Just when it seemed that no new wild lilies were to be found, the regal lily, *L. regale,* made its debut in 1904, having been imported to Europe and North America from the China-Tibet border. It is now considered the standard for white garden lilies and has an intoxicating aroma.

The tiger lily, *L. lanciflorum,* grows wild in Korea, China, and Japan, where it has been revered for its beauty and grown for its delicate flavor for at least 2,000 years. Considered a symbol of war by the Orientals, it was first brought to Europe in 1804 by plant collector William Kerr.

The last lilies to bloom during the season are the gold-banded lilies, *L. auratum,* which have fragrant, slightly drooping white flowers with crimson spots and a central gold stripe on each petal, and the Oriental hybrids, with flowers of yellow, white, pink, or red. When interest in other lilies started to wane during the nineteenth century in Europe, the introduction of the gold-banded lily from Japan caused a revival of interest in these bulbs. The gold-banded lily became one of the parents of the Oriental hybrids, which were bred, despite their name, in the U.S., Australia, and New Zealand.

Lilies make excellent cut flower arrangements (although many flower arrangers remove the golden-colored stamens to prevent staining the furniture). The lily is a popular florists' flower as well. At the famous Dutch flower auction in Aalsmere near Amsterdam, more than 200 million stems are bought every year, representing only a fraction of all the cut lilies sold in the world. The lily has become such a worldwide favorite that lily societies have sprung up all over the world—in the U.S., Canada, Australia, Czechoslovakia, Denmark, England, France, Germany, New Zealand, Poland, South Africa, Sweden, and the U.S.S.R.

Shakespeare gave the highest praise to the colors of the lily (as well as to the scent of violets) when he wrote: "To gild refined gold, to paint the lily, to throw perfume on the violet, is wasteful and ridiculous excess."

MAGNOLIA

The magnolia is one of the world's oldest plants; fossils of the plant have been found that date back 100 million years. At one time, it was believed that the magnolia, named after the French botanist Pierre Magnol, was the ancestor of all flowering plants and was the first plant whose seeds were formed in a protective fruit. This theory was recently disproved with the discovery of the oldest known flower fossil, which dates back 120 million years and is not a magnolia. Nevertheless, the importance of the magnolia in plant evolution cannot be stressed enough.

The earliest cultivated magnolia is the Chinese *M. denudata,* which has pure white, scented petals and is sometimes called the lily tree. At one time, its buds were preserved and used in medicines and to flavor rice. It was first introduced into Europe in 1789, after which it was taken to North America. Europeans were aware of other magnolias by this time. *M. kobus* had arrived by 1709. It is a small Japanese tree that does not produce its slightly fragrant, white flowers until it is about 12 to 15 years old.

Asia is the source of some of the most prized garden magnolias. Star magnolia, *M. stellata,* explodes into bloom in early spring with flowers made up of a multitude of strap-shaped petals. The saucer magnolia, *M. soulangeana,* is magnificent, with flowers of white or pink that are often tinged with purple. It was named for Mr. Soulange-Bodin, who originally raised it outside Paris during the early nineteenth century. *M. pumila,* the dwarf magnolia from the mountains of Amboyna, has deliciously scented flowers that pleased European gardeners when it was introduced in 1786.

Three magnolia species are native to India. The most magnificent is *M. campbellii,* which, at 150 feet in height and 12 feet in width, forms a conspicuous feature in the scenery of Darjeeling. Sometimes called the pink tulip tree, this magnolia can have many hundreds of large, pink flowers in bloom on one tree at one time in early spring.

Unfortunately, pink tulip trees have to be 20 to 30 years old before they bloom. After its introduction into England, it became the subject of much hybridizing during the twentieth century.

Of the 35 or so species of magnolia, eight are native to the eastern U.S. They are prized for their large, white flowers, conelike fruits and large leaves. One of the most magnificent is the southern magnolia, *Magnolia grandiflora,* whose large glossy leaves and huge fragrant flowers have won it the titles of state tree and flower of Mississippi and the state flower of Louisiana. It has very hard wood often used to make crates and boxes. Europeans started growing this plant after it was sent from the U.S. in 1734.

However large the southern magnolia may be, it is outsized by the bigleaf magnolia, *M. macrophylla,* whose flower is the largest of any U.S. native and whose 30-inch leaf is the largest undivided leaf anywhere in the world. The Chinese *M. delavayi* is the largest-leaved of the Oriental species. Smaller-flowered, sweet bay, or swamp magnolia, *M. virginiana,* was the first American magnolia taken to Europe, in 1688. Its wood is soft and is used to make handles, novelties, and inexpensive furniture.

The cucumber tree, *M. acuminata,* is named for the shape of the fruit. Its yellow wood is similar to poplar and is used to make bowls. It was first taken to Europe in 1736. A variety of this plant known as *cordata* was lost in the wild for over 100 years when it was rediscovered in Georgia in 1913. The umbrella tree, *M. tripetala,* is so named because the leaves at the ends of the branches are arranged like the ribs of an umbrella. Introduced to England in 1752, it has flowers with a strong, pleasing scent.

Two native American species, *M. tripetala* and *M. virginiana,* mated in England in the early 1800's to form *M. X thompsoniana,* a hybrid species with large, fragrant, parchment-colored flowers that bloom throughout the summer.

East met West when Dr. Todd Gresham, a noted magnolia enthusiast from Santa Cruz, California, produced a series of crosses known as the Gresham hybrids in the 1950's. He relied primarily on Oriental species.

MARIGOLD

Native to the New World from Argentina north through New Mexico and Arizona, marigolds crossed the Atlantic twice to become one of the U.S.'s most popular annual flowers. The earliest recorded use of the marigold was by the Aztecs, who attributed magical, religious, and medicinal properties to it. Reference to it appears in the De La Crus-Badiano Aztec Herbal of 1552, which recommends *Tagetes lucida* for the treatment of hiccups, lightning strikes, or "for one who wishes to cross a river or water safely."

The Aztecs named their native flower *cempoalxochitl* and bred it for increasingly large flowers. It is believed that the Spanish explorer Cortez took seeds to Spain, where plants were cultivated in monastery gardens. From Spain, marigold seeds were transported to France, England, and northern Africa, and plants soon became naturalized. During a 1535 expedition by Charles V of France to conquer Tunis, the African marigolds were mistaken for native wildflowers, and for about 200 years were called *Flos africanus.* These taller marigolds, *T. erecta,* are still called African marigolds, although some devotees are trying to change the name to American marigolds.

The smaller growing marigolds, *T. patula,* are known as French marigolds, although no one is quite sure why, since they too have American origins. Their early popularity in France is undeniable. In fact, when the Huguenot refugees left France for England in 1573, they took these marigolds with them. Early gardeners believed that the yellow blooms were streaked in red to commemorate the blood shed by the Aztecs when the Spanish conquered them. For this reason, the marigold has been called the flower of death.

Crosses between the French and African marigolds, first achieved in 1939, are technically known as triploids and informally known as mules. Like mules, they cannot reproduce, and so they put all of their energy into flowering. Both French and triploid marigolds have varieties with red flowers, a color not yet known among African marigolds.

The Latin name for the marigold genus, *Tagetes,* traces back to the revered Italian god, Tages. A grandson of Jupiter, Tages came forth from a clod of earth as a wise and handsome boy and was famed for his beauty. A second theory of the origin of the name stems from the French word *tagé,* meaning "principality," which shows the importance the French gave to the flower.

Marigolds are an intrinsic part of several religious ceremonies. In Mexico and Latin America, marigold flowers are used to decorate household altars to celebrate All Saints Day and All Souls Day, and are a common funeral flower. Devout Spanish Catholics placed the marigold on altars of the Virgin Mary, hence the name Mary's Gold, which later became marigold. The Hindus call the African marigold *gendha* and use it in garlands to decorate village gods during the harvest festival. Leis made of marigolds are also a symbol of friendship in India, and the flowers are used as a yellow cloth dye in India and Pakistan.

Shortly after the American Revolution, marigolds were reintroduced from Europe to the continent of their origin.

Around 1900, sweet peas and asters were the most popular flowers in the U.S. Unfortunately, both of them were becoming beleaguered by diseases and declining overall performance. The time was right for a "new" flower. In 1915 David Burpee took over the seed company which was founded by his father, W. Altee Burpee and, until his death in 1980, was the leading force in the promotion of marigolds. Since Burpee got the ball rolling, more time and money have been spent on improving the marigold than on any other garden annual. In 1939, the first hybrid flower from seed to be offered for commercial sale in the U.S. was Burpee's Red and Gold marigold.

David Burpee, known as D.B. to his colleagues, was a man of wit and wisdom. He commented about the development of the first hybrid flower seed, saying, "I am shocked when I reflect on how long it took the human race to get around to accomplishing this.

The first hybrid known to man was the mule, a cross between the jackass and the mare. That was many thousands of years ago and I believe it was the jackass' own idea."

One of Burpee's goals was the development of a white-flowered marigold. In 1975, after 56 years of research, the white marigold was achieved by an amateur breeder, Mrs. Alice Vonk of Sully, Iowa, who received $10,000 for her efforts. Named Snowbird, this breakthrough in the flower color of African marigolds is still being sought in French marigolds and triploids.

Certain varieties of marigolds are grown in Mexico and the southwestern U.S. specifically for adding to poultry feeds to enhance the color of egg yolks to a golden yellow. The pigment xanthophyll also produces creamy colored "white" meat when fed to poultry.

Marigold leaves have a pungent, spicy odor. They have been used to heal wounds and cure warts. Although odorless varieties are available, they are not very popular (except with flower arrangers), a great surprise to the scientists who bred the odor out.

Although the rose won as the National Floral Emblem in 1988, the marigold came in a close second. Aided by the Marigold Society of America, which was founded in 1978, this garden beauty has received much recognition. Thanks to the society's efforts, 1987 was declared the Year of the Marigold by the National Garden Bureau.

NASTURTIUM

The dwarf nasturtium, *Tropaeolum minor,* was first found growing in Mexico and Peru where it was used instead of cress to flavor foods. There is also reference to its use as an edible plant among ancient Persians. It was known in the New World as *capuchina,* meaning "little hood," because of the shape of the yellow, red, or orange flowers. During the sixteenth century, Dr. Nicholas Monardes, a physician, scholar, and author from Seville, Spain, grew nasturtiums from seeds brought to him from Peru. He called them Flowers of Blood.

Monardes shared his seeds with Jean Robin, keeper of the king's garden in Paris, and by the late seventeenth century, during the reign of Louis XIV, nasturtiums had become very popular. Le Notre, Louis' landscape architect, used the plant in formal patterned garden beds.

By 1575, the English had received seeds from France and had discovered the tartness of the nasturtium leaf, calling the plant Indian cress because its flavor resembled that of watercress. John Parkinson, gardener, apothecary, and botanist to King Charles I, described nasturtiums as "the prettiest flower of a score in a garden," but mistakenly thought it was related to the delphinium because of the spurred flowers.

Sailors of the day took barrels of pickled nasturtium seeds on long voyages, eating them like capers to prevent scurvy. They didn't know it at the time, but they were eating the wrong part of the plant; the leaves are much higher in vitamin C. Nasturtium flowers were also eaten during this period to soften the muscles and keep them from becoming stiff. Oil from the seeds was often rubbed over the body after exercising for the same reason.

The nasturtium returned to American soil with the first English colonists, and it is still so popular that it is one of the top ten garden flowers grown from seed today.

T. majus, a climbing relative of *T. minor,* was introduced in 1684. Because of its vining habit, botanists of the day thought it was related to the morning glory. Flowers of both species were very popular in nosegays and tussie mussies and were used in the Victorian era to symbolize conquest and victory in battles.

A close relative, the canary flower or canary creeper, *T. canariensis,* is a rapid-growing vine. It was first discovered in Lima, Peru, and reached Britain about 1750. It was not named for the Canary Islands, once thought to be its native land, but for the canary bird, which is the same color as its yellow flowers.

The genus name for nasturtiums, *Tropaeolum,* may originate from the Greek word meaning "to twine." Another theory traces its origin from the latin word *tropaeum,* which was a trophy presented at Roman triumphs. To the botanists of the sixteenth century who first named the plant, the round leaf suggested a shield and the flower a spear-pierced, blood-stained golden helmet.

The word nasturtium itself is a combination of the Latin word *nasus,* meaning nose, and *tortum,* meaning twist. It may have been dubbed a "nose twister" because the mustard oil contained in the leaves could bring a grimace to the face of the person smelling it. The peppery flavor of the nasturtium is still popular today, and the leaves, flowers, and fresh or pickled flower buds can be used in salads, sandwiches, and as garnish (eating fresh seeds is no longer recommended because of their high oxalic acid content).

Easy to grow and flourishing in the poorest of soil, nasturtiums are a favorite of gardeners everywhere, so much so that the National Garden Bureau named 1990 as the Year of the Nasturtium.

PANSY

Known as the princess of spring flowers, pansies can endure severe weather most other plants can't. When the first dry days of spring come along, gardeners rush out and buy a basket of pansy plants, and the shivering little things bud and bloom despite freezing weather, rain, or snow. Incredibly, they'll bloom nonstop from Easter to Thanksgiving.

Members of the genus *Viola,* pansies are cousins of violas, johnny-jump-ups, and many species of violets. Painted faces grace johnny-jump-ups and other pansy flowers, whereas violas and violets are usually colored in pure, clear hues. All are native to temperate regions all over the world.

The pansy has a rich and diverse folklore. The faces created by the patterns on the petals, always a delight to children, have given rise to such names as monkey faces, peeping Tom, and three-faces-in-a-hood. The three petals at the front of the flower were at one time thought to represent the Christian doctrine of the Trinity, and so the flower was sometimes called herb trinity, especially in Italy.

Another name for the pansy is stepmother flower. According to Scottish and German folktales, the large lower petal is the stepmother; the two large petals to either side, the well-dressed daughters; and the two small upper petals, the poor and neglected stepdaughters. It's a wonder someone didn't think to call it Cinderella plant. The Greeks called it flame flower because the colors of the flowers are those of the flames of burning wood.

Pansies have always been associated with thoughts of romance. Its supposed magical love powers resulted in names such as cull-me-to-you, tickle-me-fancy, love-in-idleness, kiss-her-in-the-pantry, and heartsease. The Celts used its dried leaves to make a love potion—the heart-shaped leaves were thought to cure a broken heart. Nicholas Culpepper, a seventeenth-century British writer, wrote that syrup from the flowers was used to cure venereal disease.

Another very old legend says that originally all pansies were white, and only when pierced by Cupid's arrow did they become marked with purple and yellow. It was the colors that first brought the suggestion of magical love powers; Shakespeare described the pansy as "before milk-white, now purple with love's wound." He also wrote of its amorous powers in *A Midsummer Night's Dream,* "the juice of it, on sleeping eyelids laid, will make a man or woman madly dote upon the next live creature that it sees." In *Hamlet,* Ophelia says, "and there is pansies, that's for thoughts."

John Milton, the seventeenth-century English poet, wrote of "Pansies and violets, and asphodel, and hyacinth, earth's freshest, softest lap."

The name pansy comes from the French noun *pensée,* which means "thought," and the verb *penser,* which means "to think" (both are pronounced pon-say). Before Elizabethan times (late-sixteenth century), the English called it boneset. The French believed that the pansy could make your lover think of you, so the name was accepted by the romantic poets of the period. The three colors of the original pansy—purple, yellow, and white—were said to symbolize memories, loving thoughts, and souvenirs, all things to ease the hearts of separated lovers. It was, however, considered bad luck for a woman to give pansies to a man.

It is said that the Knights of the Round Table used pansies to predict the future. Studying the lines on the petals, they believed that four lines meant hope; seven, constancy in love; eight, fickleness; nine, changing of the heart; eleven, disappointment in love and an early death. If the lines were thick and skewed to the left, it meant a life of trouble; when they were slanted to the right, it predicted prosperity to the end. If the center line was the longest, marriage was impending, and Sunday would be the wedding day.

Not all folktales about pansies are pleasant; according to English superstition, to pick a pansy with dew on it will cause the death of a loved one.

It is the wildflower johnny-jump-up or wild pansy, *V. tricolor,* crossed with the great yellow pansy, *V. lutea,* that is the predecessor of today's hybrid pansy, *V. X wittrockiana,* a biennial plant usually grown as a garden annual. The johnny-jump-ups, tiny-flowered plants with faces of purple, white, and yellow, were the subject of dedicated study in the early nineteenth century by an English gardener named Thompson and his cooperative employer, Lord Gambier, a British naval commander. Thompson experimented with johnny-jump-ups for 30 years, finally creating a flower that retained the lively charm and coloration of the small wildflower but had the size and beauty to please the fussiest gardener. The spur in the flower that is characteristic of the violet family was lost, and large, flat petals became the norm.

At the same time, working independently, Lady Mary Bennett and her gardener, Mr. Richardson, developed similar crosses between *V. tricolor* and *V. lutea.* The English florists quickly exploited this new flower and, between 1835 and 1838, there were 400 recorded varieties of what were then called show pansies. The show pansies made their way to France and Belgium, where they developed more strongly blotched petals. When they returned to England about 1850, the British called these new flowers fancy pansies. Few varieties of show pansies or fancy pansies remain today.

Now seed catalogs separate pansies into multiflora and grandiflora types. The grandiflora strains have the largest flowers, whereas the multiflora types have smaller flowers, but more of them. Plant breeders of the late twentieth century have been concentrating on increasing the pansy's intolerance to heat, with U.S. efforts led by the Goldsmith Seed Company in Gilroy, California, and the Harris Moran Seed Company of Rochester, New York. Excellent breeding is also being done by two overseas seed companies: Sakata in Japan and Sluis and Groot in Holland.

Both the leaves and the flowers of pansies are edible and have a high content of vitamins A and C. The flowers have a strong flavor and have been used to make syrup, honey, and custard, and are even sometimes candied. Both leaves and flowers can be used as garnish on cold fruits, salads, and soups. The flowers are sometime used in dyes.

Unfortunately, pansies still tend to die out when hot summer weather starts to set in, but their brightly colored blooms do cheerful wonders to lift the spirits on a wet, dreary day in fall, southern winters, or spring.

PEONY

The peony was named for Paeon, the physician to the Greek gods and a student of Asclepius, the god of medicine and healing. There are two different myths about how the peony came to be. One states that Paeon had found the peony to be a remedy for the pain of childbirth. The other attributes Paeon's using the peony root to cure Pluto of a wound inflicted by Hercules during the Trojan War. In each story, Asclepius became jealous and angry with Paeon and threatened to kill him. To protect him, Zeus changed Paeon into the peony flower.

The Greeks took the peony as a symbol of healing. Peony seeds have been given to pregnant women for centuries. The peony has been called the blessed herb and has been used through the ages for many medicinal reasons: healing wounds, curing insanity, preventing epilepsy, soothing toothaches, healing jaundice, and soothing stomach pains.

Peonies were also believed to have magical virtues, including the ability to protect shepherds and their flocks, to ward off storms and nightmares, and to protect the harvest. Mothers hung strings of peony seeds around their babies' necks to prevent eye disease. Seeds were also used as protection against witchcraft, demons, and the devil. Roots and seeds were gathered at night because some plants glowed in the dark.

The peony has grown in China for over 2,000 years. The Chinese call it sho-yo, which means "most beautiful," and consider it a flower of prosperity. According to the Chinese calendar, the tree peony is the floral symbol for March.

The Japanese treasure the peony as a symbol of a happy marriage and virility. It is the Japanese floral emblem for the month of June, the traditional month for weddings. The peony was the source of inspiration for both ancient Chinese and Japanese songs and poems.

There once was a country named *Paeonia,* the botanical name for the peony. The only country ever to be named for a flower, it was located in what is now northern Greece and was conquered during the Persian War.

The first peonies in northern Europe were brought there from southern Europe by the Roman legions by 1000 A.D. Cherished at first for their medicinal qualities, then as seasonings, they were admired as a European garden plant by the 1700's (the Chinese and Japanese had realized the ornamental value of the peony for over 700 years).

Double-flowered peonies, *P. officinalis,* were growing in the Mediterranean by at least the fifteenth century and were introduced into England in the sixteenth century. Also called the female peony *(P. feminea), P. officinalis,* the peony of mythology, originally had a single red flower, although it is the double form that is best known today. Single and double whites and then pinks followed the reds. The male peony, *P. mascula,* which was established in Europe by at least the twelfth century, had deep purple, red, pink, and white flowers. It is very rare today.

The first fragrant peonies in the western world came with the introduction of *P. lactiflora* (once called *P. albiflora*) at the end of the eighteenth century. It was brought back by a traveler in Russia who found the Mongols eating its roots like potatoes and using its seeds in teas. The peony was exported from China to Japan by the eighth century and was hybridized by 1000 A.D.

It was also about the end of the eighteenth century that the tree peony, *P. suffruticosa,* was introduced into Europe from the Orient. The tree peony dates back to ancient China and was exported to Japan in 724 A.D. Unlike herbaceous peonies, whose stems die to the ground each winter, the tree peony is a woody plant and often has much larger and showier flowers.

During the early nineteenth century, French hybridizers crossed *P. officinalis* and several other species of peonies with *P. lactiflora* and created a number of large-flowered, scented plants, some of which are still available today. The British, led by James Kelway, were hybridizing by the 1860's, and the U.S. by the early 1900's.

The peony was introduced to the U.S. by the early colonists, and for the Philadelphia Centennial Exposition in 1876, it was used as a symbol of American spirit, ambition, and determination.

Although the rose has been dubbed the Queen of the Flowers, it is the peony that has been called the King of the Flowers. Single or double flowered, with some blooms larger than a dinner plate, the peony has always been and will remain one of the most important flowers to adorn the late spring perennial garden.

PETUNIA

The evolution of the petunia as a garden plant is shrouded in mystery and speculation. In fact, there are two perfectly plausible explanations for the origin of the name. Liberty Hyde Bailey, a famous horticulturist who lived from 1858 to 1954, attributes the name to a French botanist named Petun who collected seeds in Argentina and returned with them to France in the 1850's. Other horticulturists and historians give credit to Antoine Laurent Jussieu, who Latinized the Brazilian petun or pety, which means "tobacco" (the petunia is a close relative of tobacco). Petunias are also closely related to potatoes, tomatoes, and peppers.

Whatever the derivation of the name, it is known that petunias were growing in private and botanical gardens by the mid-1800's, brought to Europe from South America. The earliest records date plants from Brazil reaching Europe by 1823 and from Argentina in 1831. Spanish explorers found petunias growing in Argentina in the sixteenth century, but didn't feel that the trailing plant with fragrant white flowers was worth taking back to the Continent.

Today's petunias find their ancestry in two species: *P. violacea,* a floppy 12-inch perennial with small, tubular flowers of pinkish red or reddish violet, and *P. axillaris,* a two-footer whose flowers are dull white and intensely fragrant. Both parents have given their offspring sticky, hairy leaves. Other species that may have contributed to modern petunias are *P. nyctaginiflora,* believed to be the source of fragrance in petunias, and *P. integrifolia.*

It is not known whether the earliest hybridization between petunia species was accidental or by design, but it is known that plant breeders in France, Belgium, Britain, and Germany were making crosses by the mid-nineteenth century. A major breakthrough came in 1849 when the first double-flowered petunias were developed. Across the Atlantic shores, Mrs. Theodosia Shepherd was breeding petunias in California as early as 1880. Her efforts were known as Superbissima types, which remained popular until the 1930's. By the end of the nineteenth century, petunias in all their forms—single, double, grandiflora, and multiflora—were known.

All of these forms are still popular today, the grandiflora for its large flowers and the multiflora for its abundance of smaller flowers and increased disease resistance. Petunias are available in every color of the rainbow, their trumpet-shaped single or powderpuff-shaped double flowers often splashed, starred, edged, speckled, striped, or veined in a contrasting color. Some petunias have fringed petals, a trait that first came on the scene in the 1930's.

Petunias began to fall out of favor in Europe by the late 1800's, as geraniums were becoming the plant in vogue. It was the hybridizers, mostly in North America, who took over and put the petunia where it is today. Petunias still rank in the top three flowering annual plants and fill gardens, window boxes, and hanging baskets with profusions of color. Some petunias, especially blue ones, have a delightful fragrance, whereas others, notably the single pinks, color gardens in the most hot and dry weather.

The development and growth of the petunia led to other breakthroughs in the plant world. Until F1 hybrids were developed, petunias (and many other plants) could not be guaranteed to come true to type or color from seed. Breeders discovered the efficacy of inbreeding and individual plant selection in the 1920's and 1930's, and, working largely with petunias, were able to attain trueness from seed for all types by 1940. The hybrid grandiflora double, introduced by Mr. T. Sakata of Japan in the early 1930's, was the first hybrid flower seed to gain any economic importance. Its price was almost seven times as high as the price of nonhybrids. The success of this flower proved that people would pay outrageously high prices for a product they desired. In the early 1950's, the first hybrid singles were being seen in seed catalogs.

Other individuals in the petunia's history include Elizabeth Bodger of Bodger Seeds in California, who wrote in 1937 that "petunias are the God-given messengers of beauty in an otherwise barren garden." Her contemporary, Ernst Benary of Erfurt, Germany, was the first to develop a line of dwarf, fringed petunias that were named for his home town.

In 1941, David Burpee, the leading seedman of the time, took an interest in promoting petunias, even though marigolds were always his favorite. When Sakata's production facilities were destroyed during World War II, the only double-flowered grandiflora petunias on the American market were the result of the breeding efforts of Robert Simonet of Edmonton, Alberta, Canada. His variety, America, was the first double petunia to be bred in North America.

The Pan American Seed Company, currently headquartered in suburban Chicago, took a strong hold on the market before Mr. Sakata was able to restore his business and was soon joined in petunia-breeding efforts by the Goldsmith Seed Company of Gilroy, California (the town that holds the distinction of being the garlic capital of the world).

Petunias had an impact on the greenhouse industry and were in all probability the beginning of the spring plant business. Because petunia seeds are very small and difficult for the amateur to handle, gardeners often turned to professional growers to supply their plants. Until trueness from seed could be guaranteed, many petunias were grown from greenhouse cuttings. When greenhouse growers developed a better state of the art in presenting the bedding plant to the consumer, a real revolution in growing and marketing flowering annual plants was sparked.

Today, only impatiens and geraniums account for higher sales than petunias in the garden centers of North America; during the 1970's, petunias were the top seller.

PHLOX

The phlox crossed the Atlantic Ocean twice before it became established as one of the most popular flowering plants for the U.S. garden. Native to North America, the phlox was taken to Europe early in the eighteenth century, where it was cultivated and later reintroduced to American gardens. Breeding began in France in 1839 and in England and the U.S. early in the twentieth century.

To many, the phlox is the stately perennial, *Phlox paniculata,* that fills the late summer garden with clusters of purple, pink, red, white, salmon, and lilac flowers. This phlox, however, has many relatives that bloom in spring rock gardens and summer annual borders. The blue phlox, *P. divaricata,* fills spring gardens with color as it spreads across the ground, as do the creeping phlox, *P. stolonifera,* and *P. subulata,* which are commonly known as moss pink or mountain pink. Moss pink was first sent to Europe from the Philadelphia plant collector John Bartram in 1745; it received most of its attention 100 years later. Creeping phlox was first brought to Europe in 1800.

P. drummondii, the annual phlox, is sometimes called Texas pride for its home state and is used for low borders and edgings. The only annual phlox, it too made its way to Europe in the early 1800's and was reexported to North America by the end of that century.

All of the 60 species of phlox are native to North America, and *P. sibirica* is found in both Alaska and Siberia. Although no species are native to Hawaii or New England, garden-grown plants have spread to the wild in both places, so phlox are found in all 50 states as well as in Canada and Mexico.

Botanists describe the flower shape of phlox as salverform (tray-shaped), to describe the flat surface formed by the five petals at the end of a narrow tube.

Pliny, the first-century Roman author, wrote of a flower the Greeks used in their garlands that they called phlox. It is doubtful that this is the same plant, because phlox is native to North America. The word phlox is derived from a Greek word meaning "flame," given because many of the plant's flowers were red. Although many differently colored hybrids of garden phlox have been developed, the flowers often revert to their original purplish red color when seeds from these plants are allowed to grow.

Phlox blossoms were sent in bouquets and tussie mussies in Victorian England as love messages and wishes for sweet dreams.

The leaves of the phlox plant were sometimes crushed and mixed with water to cure skin disorders, abdominal pain, and eye problems; phlox leaves were also used as a laxative.

Although phlox in their different forms are part of the backbone of the garden today, there is little lore and legend connected with this plant. It is just too new to the plant world.

POPPY

"In Flanders Fields the poppies grow,"—that line, immortalized by John McCrae, no doubt is the first thing that springs to mind when one reflects on this plant. The poppy of Flanders Fields, the corn poppy, *Papaver rhoeas,* sprang into bloom after World War I as the famous battlefield recovered from its trampling. Since that time, the poppy has been used to commemorate those who died in wars, with small reddish-orange paper flowers appearing on lapels on Memorial Day. The first Poppy Day was celebrated in England in 1921.

The corn poppy is also called the field poppy, and its flowers are used medicinally. Unlike the narcotic opium poppy, *P. somniferum,* the corn poppy contains a nonpoisonous substance called rhoeadine that is used as a mild sedative. Its petals can be steeped in hot water and the solution used as a skin freshener—some believe it will prevent wrinkles. The petals are also used in dye to color wine, ink, and medicine.

Hybrids of the corn poppy were developed by the Dutch during the eighteenth century. A century later, crossing the Dutch poppies with one that he found growing in his garden at Shirley, England, Rev. William Wilks developed a strain that would later be called the Shirley poppy. It is characterized by the lack of the usual black blotch that appears at the base of the petals of other poppies.

Poppies have been grown for centuries for their beauty, magic, and medicine. The Egyptians felt that they were a necessary part of funerals and burial rites and that they assured life after death. Dried poppy petals have been found in tombs at least 3,000 years old. The Romans used the juice from the poppy plant to ease the pains of love. The ancient Greeks placed garlands of poppy flowers at the shrines of Demeter, the goddess of the harvest because of Demeter's grief at her daughter Persephone's abduction; this flower of grief is associated with fall and winter losses. They also used poppy seeds as a love charm and for seasonings in breads, cakes, and drinks, a practice still carried on today. Greek Olympic athletes drank a mixture of honey, wine, and poppy seeds to bring them strength and health.

In the Middle Ages, tea made from poppy petals was given to children suffering from colic or whooping cough. Adults drank poppy syrup to relieve pain, induce sleep, and cure rheumatism.

Poppies are Old World natives, growing wild in fields across Europe and Asia. The Iceland or Arctic poppy, *P. nudicaule,* grows on tundras well above the tree line, and the Oriental poppy, *P. orientale,* can be found in southwest Asia. Revered by the Chinese, the Oriental poppy is their floral emblem for December and a symbol of consolation, sleep, rest, and repose. The Oriental poppy was first brought to Europe around the start of the eighteenth century.

There are several theories about the origin of the genus name for the poppy, *Papaver.* One is from pap, a ground food that often contained the juice of poppies, given to infants to help them sleep. Another is from the Celtic word that described the sound made by the Roman soldiers when they ate poppy seeds.

There are many other plants called poppies. Although they are in the same family, they are not in the same genus. The California poppy, *Eschscholzia californica,* is the state flower of California and fills its hillsides with gold in the spring. The blue poppy, *Meconopsis betonicifolia,* is one of the only poppies not brightly colored orange, red, pink, or yellow. The prickly poppies in the *Argemone* genus are armed with stiff spines and are native to the harsh desert climate of the southwest U.S. and northern Mexico.

Poppy flowers are fleeting, but they are quickly replaced by others. Robert Burns, the eighteenth-century Scottish poet, summed up this bloom in his words: "Pleasures are like poppies spread, you seize the flower, its bloom is shed."

PRIMROSE

The name for the primrose genus, *Primula,* is from the Latin word *primus,* which means "first." It was given to this plant because it is one of the first to bloom in spring. Native to cool, moist meadows, and shady woodlands, the primrose blooms in generally brightly colored clusters of flowers above rosettes of crinkled, light green leaves.

The primrose is rich in symbolism. It has been taken to mean youth, and a walk down the primrose path means a life of pleasure and self-indulgence. A song from the early 1960's proclaimed that "life's a holiday on primrose lane." In English folk legends, the primrose was a sign of being pampered. The word primrose was also associated with excellence.

There are many common names for the primrose. The translation of the German word for primrose means "little keys to heaven." According to legend, St. Peter heard about some wayward souls that were trying to sneak into heaven through the back door instead of the pearly gates. He became upset and dropped the keys to heaven, and where they landed on earth, primroses grew.

Additionally, some see a resemblance between the flower clusters and a bunch of keys. It was once believed that the primrose had the magical power to open treasure chests or to open rocks that would reveal treasures. Such myth-related names for the primrose are Our Lady's key, marriage key, key flower, Virgin's keys, and St. Peter's keys.

Other common names for the primrose allude to their mystical connections and include such titles as fairy flower, fairy cup, or fairy basins. The primrose most often called fairy primrose is *P. malacoides,* an annual that has loose clusters of rose, lavender, or white flowers. Fairies were thought to take shelter under the primrose's leaves during rain showers.

Cowslip is a popular English name for a perfumed primrose, *P. veris.* The derivation of its name is uncertain, but one theory is that it came from the words cow slop. Because primroses once grew so abundantly in grazing fields, the superstition arose that they grew from cow dung. Even though its origins may seem unpleasing, it has been a treasured flower for centuries and was mentioned by Shakespeare in many of his works.

Primroses are a large genus of perennials and annuals. One of the oldest species is *P. auricula,* which has very hairy leaves and richly fragrant flowers. They were first mentioned in the first-century writings of Dioscorides. Especially popular in England, where they were introduced in 1575, they were a common subject of poets of the time. Striped flowers, which have all but disappeared, were known by the mid-1650's, and green- and white-edged types were known by the mid-1700's.

Other common species include the German primrose, *P. obconica,* which has fragrant flowers of purple, pink, red, or white, and rough, hairy leaves that often cause a rash. The Japanese primrose, *P. japonica,* has unique blooms that appear in clustered intervals along the stem and is known as a candelabra type. It was first introduced to Europe from Japan in 1870.

The original English primrose, *P. vulgaris,* has pale yellow flowers and was immortalized by Shakespeare, Keats, Spencer, Chaucer, and Milton because of its free-flowering simplicity. The double-flowered and white-flowered varieties were known as early as 1500; reds and pinks were brought to western Europe from Greece, the Caucasus, and Persia by 1635. The first reference to a blue flower appeared in 1648.

The florists' primrose, polyanthus primrose, *P. X polyanthus,* a hybrid between the cowslip and the English primrose since at least the sixteenth century, is the brightest of all. It has blooms of white, purple, blue, red, pink, or yellow, often with a marked contrasting center. They were first grown in England and were popular in North America by the early eighteenth century.

From the mid-eighteenth to the mid-nineteenth centuries, the only primroses thought worthy of attention were the gold- and silver-laced sorts. These had dark flowers, and each lobe of the flower was outlined with a narrow band of yellow or white that looped down into the center of the flower and divided it into ten perfectly even portions. Their popularity declined by the mid-nineteenth century, however, and gardeners turned to double sorts and varieties with large flowers. In 1870, Gertrude Jeckyll found a yellow polyanthus in her garden that started the famous Munstead strain in which white and yellow flowers predominated.

In medieval times the primrose was considered to be a cure for gout and a remedy for lost speech. Mountain climbers have carried it for its supposed power to combat altitude sickness. It has also been used for convulsions, hysteria, neck and muscular pain, and coughs. Water distilled from the leaves and flowers was used for head colds, dogbites, and labor pains, and an ointment made from the leaves was used for burns and skin irritations.

Cosmetics have also relied upon the primrose. Creams or distilled water made from primroses were used to keep the face beautiful and remove spots or wrinkles. The crinkled leaves were rubbed on the cheeks instead of rouge to give them a healthy red glow.

The leaves and flowers of primroses can be used fresh in salads, or mixed with other herbs as poultry stuffing. They have also been used in tea, wine, jam, jelly, preserves, pickles, and egg dishes.

Since the late 1800's, England has celebrated Primrose Day each April 19. The day honors Benjamin Disraeli, the British Prime Minister until 1880. The date was his birthday; the primrose, his favorite flower. England has a particular fondness for this flower, although they are loved the world over.

ROSES

Since the dawn of mankind, roses have offered the world their delicate beauty. No other flower has been as renowned, admired, or loved. The rose is as much a native of the United States as the bald eagle; 35 rose species are indigenous. Roses have also been found growing wild as far north as Norway and Alaska and as far south as Mexico and North Africa.

Roses apparently originated in Central Asia about 60 to 70 million years ago. The Chinese cultivated them widely at least 5,000 years ago. Confucius wrote about roses growing in China's Imperial Gardens about 500 B.C.

Roses were an integral part of life for the ancient Romans, who used them in candy, wine, pudding, garlands, and rose water. *Rosa*

damascena semperflorens, Autumn Damask, thrilled them because it bloomed twice a year, the first rose known to do this. For the Romans, the rose was a symbol of secrecy—the origin of the term "sub rosa" (under the rose). Roses were used as decorations for feasts and public games, and rose festivals were not uncommon. They crowned the heads of revelers, and were offered at memorial services for the dead. Noblemen had rose gardens at their homes, and public rose gardens were favorite places of the common people.

In the period following the fall of the Roman Empire through the Renaissance, the history of the rose is clouded and incomplete. Although roses began to reappear in private gardens about 1,000 A.D., it was not until the twelfth and thirteenth centuries, when soldiers returning from the Crusades told tales of extravagant rose gardens, that interest in the rose was truly reborn. Soon, traders, diplomats, and scholars were exchanging garden plants, including roses.

Meanwhile, across the Atlantic, separate strains of wild roses were developing. The early settlers and Native Americans planted these roses in gardens, making them the first cultivated ornamental plants on the North American continent and paving the way for future development of this extraordinary flower.

A revolution in rose growing took place in Europe in the eighteenth and nineteenth centuries when the increase in foreign trade brought *Rosa chinensis,* the China Rose, to the attention of Europeans by 1792. Its repeat bloom laid the foundation for today's roses. *Rosa odorata,* the Tea Rose, followed in 1808; its foliage has a scent similar to crushed tea leaves and is mildew-resistant, however, it is not as hardy as some of the other species.

The Bourbon Rose, *Rosa X borboniana,* was brought to Europe in 1817 from the island of Réunion (known then as Bourbon) in the Indian Ocean near Madagascar. Its background is unknown, although it is probably a hybrid, the result of a cross of *Rosa chinensis* with Autumn Damask. The Bourbon Rose quickly became popular because of its recurrent bloom. The original, bright, pink Bourbon is lost, but hybrids remain, one of which is a primary source of red in today's roses.

An American contribution to the period was *Rosa noisettiana,* the Noisette Rose. An 1812 cross between *Rosa moschata,* the Musk Rose, and *Rosa chinensis,* it was named after a nurseryman named Noisette who sent it to France, where it was raised. These roses were either tender, vigorous climbers, or bushy plants.

Modern roses were well under way by 1838, when the Hybrid Perpetual was introduced. It evolved from Bourbon, Damask, China, Portland, Tea, and Noisette roses. The plants were very hardy, the flowers large and fragrant. It was not truly a perpetual bloomer as its name implies, but it did bloom more frequently than many others. The Hybrid Perpetuals remained popular until the turn of the century.

By the end of the nineteenth century, most of the elements of modern roses were present except for one—there were no Hybrid Teas that had colors in the yellow to orange range. In 1900, Pernet-Duchet introduced Soleil d'Or, a cross between a Hybrid Perpetual and a Persian Yellow, a form of *Rosa foetida,* the Austrian Rose. With this cross, a new range of rose colors came into being: gold, copper, and apricot. It was not until Tropicana was introduced in 1960 that there was an orange-red Hybrid Tea.

In 1862, French nurseryman Jean Sisley crossed *Rosa multiflora* and *Rosa chinensis minima* to produce a new class of rose known as Polyanthas. These plants were low-growing and covered in clusters of small flowers. A Danish rose breeder named Poulsen crossed the Polyantha with the Hybrid Tea in 1924 and produced the Floribunds. These plants inherited an abundance of flowers from the Polyantha, and long stems from the Hybrid Tea.

Climbing roses have complex histories and cannot easily be set into distinct patterns. Some climbers evolved from ramblers, the first of which was the 1893 Crimson Rambler, the result of a cross between *Rosa wichuriana* and *Rosa multiflora.* Other climbers are the descendants of both bush roses that produce long, pliable canes and large shrub roses.

The miniature rose is descended from *Rosa chinensis minima,* the fairy rose that reached Europe from the island of Mauritius in the Indian Ocean in 1815. It eventually disappeared from gardens and was thought to be lost, until it was rediscovered growing in a window box in Switzerland in the 1980's. It was renamed *Rosa rouletti* for the man who rediscovered it. Several breeders are presently introducing large numbers of new miniatures.

SNAPDRAGON

Children have always delighted in squeezing the bloom of the snapdragon to open its brightly colored mouth, then having the flower catch their small fingers inside. These unique blooms, which come in all colors but blue, are borne along straight stems and open from the bottom of the stem up. Of the top ten garden annual flowers, snapdragons are the only ones with spiked blooms. The shape of the flower has led to many other common names, such as toad's mouth, dog's mouth or lion's mouth.

Although some snapdragons still have "jaws," some of the newer hybrids have flowers with frills, flounces, and flares. Through cross-breeding the three-foot stems of a half century ago have been replaced in many varieties with dwarf stems only eight inches long. Breeders have also increased the snapdragon's heat resistance while altering its height and flowers.

The black seed pods of the snapdragon have been called calves'

snout, because they resemble the animal's nose. The botanical name for the snapdragon, *Antirrhinum,* also alludes to that characteristic. It is derived from two Greek words, *anti,* meaning "having superficial aspects"; and *rhinos,* meaning "snout."

The snapdragon is native to southern Europe and Sicily and has become naturalized in many areas. In the wild, the flowers are primarily pink or purple, although there are a few veined in yellow or yellow throated. These plants contributed to a strain of outstanding nineteenth-century hybrids that are now lost.

In the Mediterranean area and along the Balkan Peninsula the plants were once cultivated for their seeds, which contain high amounts of oil used as a substitute for olive oil. An old tale states that if a person were to be anointed with the oil of the snapdragon, he or she would become famous. It was also believed that the oil would ward off witchcraft and sorcery.

Few records exist of the snapdragon in medieval times, although the plant was known to the ancient Greeks and Romans. It appeared again in the sixteenth century and was described in a wide variety of colors. Striped varieties were known by the early 1700's and doubles, a century later. At that time, all snapdragons were propagated by cuttings; although this is still possible, most snapdragons today are grown from seed.

The snapdragon self-pollinates or is pollinated by the bumblebee because the honey bee is not heavy enough to open the flower to get inside. Because it can self-pollinate, it need not be fragrant. In fact, it was not until 1963 that the first scented snapdragon appeared, with the fresh aroma of cinnamon.

SWEET PEA

Sweet peas are members of the legume family, those plant wonders that take nitrogen from the air and transport it to the soil beneath, fertilizing themselves, or the plants that follow. Although not in the same genus as garden peas, they are close relatives, as are beans, clover, mimosa, honey locust, wisteria, and acacia.

Botanically known as *Lathyrus odoratus,* sweet peas are one of the few members of its genus with fragrance. First discovered in Sicily in 1697 by Father Franciscus Cupani, this annual vining plant was sent to England in 1700 to Dr. Robert Uvedale, a schoolmaster at Enfield Grammar School and an avid greenhouse gardener. Interest in it was not high, except for its perfume, because the original flowers were purple and maroon and very small, and the plants had short, weak stems. In the next hundred years, only six new varieties were developed, and the flower size was not improved except for Painted Lady, a reddish pink-and-white bicolor that is still grown today.

The flower was named sweet pea by the early nineteenth-century English poet Keats. He described them as "on tiptoe for a flight with wings of gentle flush o'er delicate white." Despite this publicity, sweet peas did not gain in popularity until later in that century. In 1870, Henry Eckford, gardener to Dr. Sankey in Gloucestershire, realized the commercial possibilities of the sweet pea and left his employment to devote full time to creating new varieties. At the Bi-Centennial Sweet Pea Exhibition held at the Crystal Palace in Sydenham in 1900, half of the 264 varieties on display had been created by Eckford. He called his sweet peas giants or grandifloras for their larger-than-normal flowers, which were nonetheless smaller than those available today.

Sweet peas were also doing more at this time than just contributing pretty flowers and rich aroma to gardens and homes. It was with this plant that Father Gregor Mendel performed his famous work in genetics.

In 1901, the National Sweet Pea Society was formed in England. Within the next decade, a sweet pea with large ruffled petals was discovered by Silas Cole, gardener to the Countess Spencer, who was the grandmother of Princess Diana. Almost overnight, these new sweet peas, called Spencers, became the rage. In time, however, they fell out of favor because they lost some of their predecessors' heat resistance and fragrance.

Soon after the discovery of the Spencers, another sweet pea with ruffled petals was found in the garden of a Cambridge grocer named Unwin. Unlike the Spencers, the Unwins would grow true from seed, so Mr. Unwin closed his grocery store and starting developing new varieties, raising sweet peas for the florists' market.

Sweet peas reached their height of popularity during this time and were considered the floral emblem for King Edward VII, who abdicated the throne in 1910. They were used extensively as a cut flower and were included in flower arrangements for all sorts of occasions. Dried petals were a common ingredient in potpourries.

By World War I, the original Sicilian sweet pea and the grandiflora had become all but unknown, and the new varieties of the day included the Cuthbertsons, which were early blooming, fragrant, and unusually heat resistant. Following in the 1920's and the 1930's were the multiflora sweet peas, which had an abundance of smaller flowers.

Next in development came the bush-type sweet peas, which culminated in the early 1980's with the development of sweet peas that have no tendrils, but leaves instead. Because they have no tendrils, they cannot climb. Snoopea, the first of these new varieties, was awarded the Silver Cup from the National Sweet Pea Society, an honor that had not been bestowed in 30 years.

New types of sweet peas developed in the 1980's have brought old favorites into the limelight again. Nostalgia lovers will be happy to hear that a California plant breeder has reintroduced the original Sicilian and grandiflora sweet peas by gathering stock from private gardens in England. Because of the wonderful fragrance, the mixture has been called Old Spice.

Blooming in a palette of pastel shades in every color save yellow, sweet peas prefer cool weather and have often been considered the flower for April.

TULIP

Although many other spring bulbs herald the coming of a new season, regal tulips indicate that spring is here to stay. Tulips share with hyacinths a formality and stateliness that has caused them to be chosen for mass plantings in parks and palaces all over the world.

No one knows for sure where or when the first tulip was discovered but, as with many other flowers, mythology plays a role. According to an ancient Persian myth, a young man named Ferhad was spurned by his lover, Sharin, and wept for his unrequited love. Each tear that fell was transformed into a tulip, the Queen of the Bulbs. Another version of the story tells that Ferhad fell to his death from a high cliff upon hearing that Sharin was dead. Tulips sprang up on the spot where his body landed. Actually, Sharin was very much alive, and Ferhad's demise was the result of a rumor spread by a jealous rival.

It is known that tulips existed before Christ, growing across southern Europe, Asia Minor, and across Asia to China. Tulip designs have been found on pottery jars dating from 2200 to 1600 B.C. It was in Turkey that many tulips have their origins, and it was a Turkish sultan, Ahmed III, whose reign from 1703 to 1730 was known as the Age of Tulips because he adorned gardens with them. The tulip was already popular in Europe, with the first known use of it occurring in a garden dating to 1559. Ogier Chislain de Busbecq, Ambassador of Emperor Ferdinand I of Austria to the Court of the Turkish Empire, brought the tulip from Turkey to northern Europe, after first seeing it in 1554.

The man who played the key role in bringing the tulip to Holland was Carolus Clusius, Prefect of the Imperial Medicinal Garden of Emperor Maximillian II in Vienna. When Maximillian died in 1576, Clusius lost his position and moved to Holland, taking with him the best of the seeds, plants, and bulbs he had grown in the Viennese garden. There are accounts of Clusius not being willing to part with his tulips and his charging such high prices for them that a band of thieves stripped his garden beds. It is also reputed that he hid the most precious bulbs under his bed. Whether these stories are true or not, Clusius certainly was the father of the bulb industry in Holland.

After its introduction, the tulip grew immensely in popularity across Europe. Between 1634 and 1637, a phenomenon occurred in Europe known as tulipomania. Speculation on this one item alone drove the prices so high that those possessed with tulipomania would trade two loads of wheat, four fat oxen, 12 fat sheep or 1,000 pounds of cheese for one tulip bulb. When the bottom fell out of the tulip market, only government intervention in the form of price freezes could bring order to the chaos and economic depression that followed. Learning from the mistakes of the Dutch, the Turkish government passed strict laws during the Age of Tulips. Bulbs could be traded only in the capital city and punishment for breaking this law was exile.

From the few hundred varieties known in the seventeenth century, there are now over 3,000 known and named tulips, with close to 1,000 still in commerce. Although some bulbs are produced elsewhere, most of the world's tulips are still grown in Holland, and the Dutch have adopted it as their national flower. Approximately 1.6 billion tulip bulbs are exported from Holland each year, almost four times the number of any other spring bulb. It would take one person over 4,300 years, planting 1,000 bulbs a day, to plant what Holland exports in one year, and that's only about 70 percent of the total produced in that country.

As with other plants, tulips have been divided into a number of classifications based on size, blooming time, and heritage. This classification system was first devised in the early 1900's by a joint effort of the Royal Horticultural Society of England and the Royal General Bulb Growers Society of Holland.

The earliest tulip to poke its head through the soil in spring is *Tulipa kaufmanniana* and its hybrids, which not surprisingly are called *Kaufmanniana* tulips. They are often called waterlily tulips because the flat flowers with white petals and yellow centers look like the aquatic plant. Most tulips will not grow and bloom where subfreezing marks are not reached in winter, but the Kaufmannianas, like many Americans, can vacation in Florida.

The next to bloom are the *Fosterianas* and many of the "species" tulips. The former, hybrids of *T. fosteriana,* have large, cup-shaped blooms often set off by striped or mottled foliage; species tulips are usually low-growing favorites for rock gardeners. The classic egg-shaped flower of the tulip first appears on the single early varieties, which are fragrant and very resistant to the ravages of weather that still plaque early spring gardens. The double early, which are full-flowered varieties are longer lasting yet.

The gap that at one time existed between early spring and late spring in the tulip garden was closed when *Triumph* tulips were created, a cross between single early and later-flowering tulips with egg-shaped flowers. Blooming at the same time are the *Greigii* tulips, the hybrids of *T. greigii* with striped or mottled foliage and flat flowers in warm-colored tones.

Crossing the late-flowering Darwins with the early-flowering Fosterianas, hybridizers created another mid-spring tulip. Instead of giving them a new name, they called them *Hybrid Darwins,* which, to say the least, causes some confusion. They look like the *Darwins,* the most popular tulips with egg-shaped flowers, but so far hybridizers have achieved only red, yellow, and orange flowers with the Hybrid Darwins. Darwins, on the other hand, come in every imaginable color from pure white to almost black.

Tulips known as *Rembrandt* tulips have vivid stripes or blotches and are known as "broken" tulips. Gardeners have planted them for centuries because of the unique colorations, but it has been only in the twentieth century that horticulturists found that the coloration is, in fact, due to a virus.

Blooming with the Darwins are the similar Cottage tulips, which are also called single late tulips. They come in many colors, except blue and purple. The viridiflora types, which do not represent a separate class, are a kind of Cottage tulip that has green streaks on the outside of the petals. Also late bloomers, the Lily tulips have long, pointed, outward-curving petals, and are joined in the garden scene by Parrots, the large-flowered kinds with fringed, feathered, and sometimes twisted petals, and the double late types which are among the most informal of this formal flower.

Any popular flower is bound to be the focus of festivals and parades, and so it is with the tulip. The grandest in the U.S. is the Tulip Time Festival held each year in Holland, Michigan, featuring Dutch dances, street scrubbing, parades, and craft shops brimming with wooden shoes and Delft plates and statuary. Others are held in Pella, Iowa, and Orange City, Iowa, both small towns with a rich Dutch heritage.

The word tulip comes from the Turkish word *tulbend* or *tuliband,* which means "turban." Early visitors to Turkey thought the flower resembled an upsidedown turban. The Turks used bulbs in love potions and they would present a tulip with a red flower as a symbol of love, a yellow flower as a sign of hopeless love, and a tulip with a black center for a heart burning with love.

Tulips are quite edible and taste somewhat like onions. The flowers are often stuffed with salads, and the central part of the flowers have been sauted in butter for a great-tasting treat.

ZINNIA

The zinnia, once a lowly wayside weed, has been transformed into one of the most colorful and spectacular of garden flowers, with blooms from wee midgets to plate-sized giants in every color of the rainbow except true blue. The first zinnias were so ugly that they were gathered only for medicinal purposes; now their descendants are a major component of summertime gardens everywhere.

Exactly who spotted the first zinnias is not known. They were noted by the Spanish explorers in Mexico in 1519, but were largely ignored; even the Aztecs called them "eyesore."

Nonetheless, seeds found their way from the temperate parts of North and Central America to Europe in the early 1750's. As it was first introduced to Europe, the zinnia had little beauty or garden potential. The species *Zinnia elegans,* the major species grown today, was then a tall, lanky plant with uninspiring daisylike flowers with a single row of stiff, purple or red petals.

The seeds of another species, *Z. peruviana,* were either imported by or given to a young German professor, Johann Gottfried Zinn, who worked at Göttingen University. They were no doubt the subject of scientific interest because plants were being studied at that time for potential use as food, fiber, or medicine, as well as for ornamental value. *Z. peruviana* is not currently used as a garden plant, but it was probably a member of the gene pool from which modern zinnias were developed. Dr. Zinn died in 1759, and because he was the "father" of this still relatively unknown plant, it was named for him in that year. As a garden plant, the zinnia remained in the background until the end of the nineteenth century when it became the subject of further experimentation and early systematic plant selection.

There were several factors that kept the zinnia from achieving the popularity it has today. In the first place, zinnias were probably hard to grow in northern Europe's cool, humid climate, since they prefer hot, dry weather and are prone to mildew during humid weather. Secondly, horticulturists and breeders were not successful in replacing the wild, single form with a true double. It was not until 1858 in India that the double zinnia became a reality.

In 1874, Haage and Schmidt, seedsmen from Erfurt, Germany, introduced a double-flowered zinnia whose flower resembled that of a dahlia. Evidently this plant did not become well known for when California's Bodger Seed Company introduced the Giant Dahlia in 1919, it was considered something new. It was this Giant Dahlia that really introduced the gardening world to the zinnia and was responsible for advancing its popularity into the ranks of the top 10 flowers of the time. The 1924 awarding of the Royal Horticultural Society of England's highest award, its Gold Medal, to Bodger's zinnia brought the entire species to the attention of the gardening public.

Although Mr. Haage's double-flowered zinnia did not make him famous, he is still remembered through *Z. haageana,* which was named for him in 1861. Commonly known today as the Mexican zinnia (it is native to Mexico), plants are characterized by double flowers that are two toned in shades of white, cream, tan, gold, and brown. Its features are about halfway between the common garden zinnia and *Z. angustifolia,* first named in 1820. This plant, sometimes called Classic zinnia, has fine-textured, narrow foliage, excellent resistance to disease, heat, and drought, and unrefined wildflower-like features.

In the first part of the twentieth century, plant breeders learned that treating plants with colchicine, a poisonous alkaloid derived from the autumn crocus, would often double a plant's chromosomes and produce new and better varieties. By 1939, Elmer Twedt of Ferry-Morse Seed Company had created tetraploids, flowers whose chromosome counts are doubled, but the introduction of the flowers was delayed by World War II. It was not until 1956 that seed catalogs carried New Century zinnias, the first tetraploid zinnia on the market. It had larger flowers, stronger stems, and increased disease resistance.

Many zinnias are known as open-pollinated flowers. With the help of insects and the wind, these plants are pollinated in fields and the seeds collected. Hybrids, on the other hand, are the result of crossing two distinctively different parents and have an edge on vigor and uniformity. They are also more expensive to produce. The first hybrid zinnia was produced for sale in 1960, 11 years after John Mondry of the Burpee Seed Company accidentally noticed a flower in a field that had all female parts, a phenomenon necessary to produce a hybrid zinnia.

Several other names have become synonymous with the zinnia. One is Youth and Old Age, referring to the zinnias' habit of opening new flower buds while mature flowers are still in their prime. As cut flowers, zinnias have earned a reputation of pouring forth new blooms and, therefore, they earned another name, Cut and Come Again. Other names occasionally used are Poorhouse Flower, a term used in the late nineteenth century in the U.S., Everybody's Flower, and Old Faithful, perhaps for its ease of culture.

Someday gardeners may be able to have blue zinnias, or fragrant zinnias, but for today they are happy with the vast array of colors and sizes already known. 1983 was the crowning year for the zinnia, for the National Garden Bureau proclaimed it the Year of the Zinnia.

True lily flowers have six petals and six anthers, and bloom atop long stems covered with long, narrow, tapered leaves. These characteristics make them easy to distinguish from many other plants that are called lilies.

Oriental hybrid lilies exhibit flower colors of yellow, white, pink, and red — sometimes in combinations.

Breeding has produced many beautiful colors in the lily, as seen in the Imperial Crimson.

The lily is one of the world's oldest plants and for centuries has been associated with mythology, religion, superstition, medicine, cosmetics, majesty, and royalty.

Following pages: *The magnolia is at least 100 million years old, making it another of the earth's oldest plants. For centuries, people have been welcomed to spring by the blooms of the saucer magnolia,* Magnolia soulangiana.

Lilium candidum, *the Madonna lily, is rich in religious symbolism. The flowers are pure white and very fragrant.*

The magnolia was one of the first plants whose seeds formed within a protective fruit. Here, a cross-section of a magnolia flower reveals the male and female parts; the seeds will form inside the red-colored area.

The summer-flowering, large, fragrant blooms of the southern magnolia, Magnolia grandiflora, have won it the designation of the State Flowers of Mississippi and Louisiana.

Magnolias of different species can be found in Asia, from the Himalayas to Japan, and the Americas, from eastern North America to Venezuela.

The original saucer magnolia had flowers that were white on the inside and purplish on the outside, but breeding has developed flowers of pure white, rose, purple, and pink.

While most magnolias are deciduous trees (losing their leaves in autumn), the southern magnolia is prized for its large, shiny, evergreen leaves.

Tagetes patula, *Happy marigolds, belong to a group known as French marigolds. The plants are excellent low-growing additions to borders, and the flowers are single, double, or crested in tones of yellow, gold, red, or mahogany.*

African marigolds, Tagetes erecta *(pictured) and French marigolds are not native to the countries their names suggest. Both are originally from the Americas, from Argentina north to Arizona and New Mexico.*

*Perfection Yellow and Perfection
Gold are new breeds of African
marigold with large flowers on
compact plants. Like all African
marigolds, they are light sensitive
and must be planted in bud or
bloom to produce flowers all
summer.*

Marigolds are grown commercially in Mexico and the southwestern U.S. as an additive for poultry feeds, because chickens that feed on the mixture produce eggs with golden yolks and creamy-colored white meat.

Many gardeners plant marigolds in their vegetable gardens to repel nematodes (a type of parasite) as well as to add color.

At present, there are no hybrid F₁ French marigolds, a goal being sought by many breeders. Another breeding goal is an African marigold with red or mahogany-colored flowers.

The nasturtium Whirlybird Mixed is a low, mounded plant with a mass of bloom carried well above the foliage; the semi-double, upward-facing flowers may be rose, gold, mahogany, orange, scarlet, tangerine, or cream.

Universally loved for its ease of growth and flowering, the nasturtium, Tropaeolum majus, is also quite at home in the salad bowl, as its leaves, flowers, and flower buds are edible and peppery in flavor.

Nasturtiums provide generous color in garden borders and hanging baskets. They thrive without care and actually grow better in poor soil or during drought.

A relative of the viola and the sweet violet, the pansy is a perky, low-growing annual, loved for the rainbow of colors it provides beginning in early spring.

A sprinkling of pansies provides an interesting contrast to a garden of purple-violet and white lobelia.

The pansy Jolly Joker won an All-American Selection award in 1990 for its unique combination of rich blue-violet upper petals and bright orange-red lower ones.

Containers planted with pansies combined with fuchsia, petunias, impatiens, and lobelia can brighten up a corner of the garden.

One of the nicest things about pansies is their versatility. Here, the purple of the pansies in this garden bed is picked up and accented by the white-and-purple pansies in the planter box.

Pansies are available in a wide range of colors, from pure white to jet black, and all colors in between.

Although many pansies are solid colored, many exhibit the characteristic "faces" that seem to smile as they nod in the breeze.

Pansies were once grown as companions for spring-flowering bulbs. Today, thanks to modern breeding, pansies have become quite heat resistant and will grow all summer in some of the hottest areas.

Like many other plants, pansies are edible. Their colorful flowers can also be used as garnish in cold summer soups for a refreshing look.

There is hardly a more rewarding
garden flower than the peony. It has
been grown in China for almost
2,500 years; most species are native
to Asia although a few have sprung
up in western North America.

It is believed that the first peonies
were red and single-flowered, which
were followed first by double reds,
then by single and double whites,
and then by pinks in both forms.

The peony Kansas is an antique
variety of peony, but it still
continues to set the standard for red
varieties among its type. Kansas
won the Gold Medal of the
American Peony Society.

One of the peony's greatest assets is
long life. Most gardeners can expect
plants to live for several decades,
and there are plants in Asian temple
gardens that are more than 100
years old.

Although most American gardeners favor double-flowered peonies, the single, or Japanese, peony has large flowers, colorful centers surrounded by glorious petals, and exceptionally strong stems.

In colonial America, the only ornamental plants many homes had was a lilac bush and a red peony, but now, new peony hybrids have produced an increased range of colors, larger flowers, and delicious fragrances.

A modern garden combines the early summer blooms of peonies, Oriental poppies, and tall bearded irises.

The common garden petunia,
Petunia X hybrida, *is a member*
of the Potato Family, Solanaceae.

Preceding pages: *America's third-favorite garden annual, the petunia, came to North America from South America via Europe. One thing today's petunia hybrids and their ancestors have in common are the sticky, hairy leaves.*

The petunia most commonly grown is the single type, with its trumpet-shaped blooms. Petunias are also available with double flowers and in every color of the rainbow.

While many petunias are solid colored, others have unique colorations. The white edging found around many different petunia flowers is known as a picotee.

Other petunias are striped in such a way that the pattern on the flower forms a star.

Petunias bloom in all colors, but the pink varieties are the most rugged and, therefore, are best to plant where the growing conditions are less than ideal.

Petunias are classified as multiflora or grandiflora types. The multiflora types have smaller flowers, but more of them; they are also more disease and weather resistant. Grandiflora petunias, which have larger flowers, are most often used in planter boxes.

The brightness of petunias makes them unrivaled in beds, borders, hanging baskets, patio containers, and window boxes.

Perennial phlox, Phlox paniculata, *is the backbone of the midsummer garden.*

The original phlox was a bright magenta, but now many varieties exist in shades of white, pink, rose, red, salmon, coral, lavender, and blue.

Phlox drummondii, *the annual phlox Beauty Blue, is native to Texas and is the only annual member of the genus.*

The crepe-papery petals of an Oriental poppy, Papaver orientale, *are about to open to reveal the flower's large, characteristic black center.*

Oriental poppies are one of the major perennials of the early summer garden. A close relative, Papaver somniferum, *opium poppy, is the source of the drug as well as of poppy seeds and an edible oil.*

The Iceland poppy, Papaver nudicaule, *is also known as the Arctic poppy because it is native to the Arctic regions of North America, Europe, and Asia.*

Poppies from the garden make excellent cut flowers when the ends of the stems are seared with a flame immediately after cutting.

The California poppy,
Eschscholzia californica,
the State Flower of California,
covers coastal hillsides with
golden waves in spring and early
summer.

*The botanical name for the
primrose,* Primula, *is from the
Latin word primus, which means
first, because the primrose is one of
the first plants to bloom in spring.*

Most of the polyanthus primroses,
Primula X polyanthus, *have
a contrasting white or yellow eye
in the center of red, pink, blue,
gold, purple, or white flowers.*

The colorful primrose is very at home in the garden, as a lawn border, or perhaps as a hedge decoration.

A true primrose lane, this garden path is pretty as well as rich in the symbolism of the primrose: pleasure, youth, and excellence.

*Almost all primroses flourish in a
cool, partially shaded environment
where the soil is rich.*

Preceding page: *Variegata di Bologna is a fragrant Bourbon rose and, although it is an old garden rose, it remains one of the finest striped roses grown.*

Class Act won the All-American Rose Selections award for 1989 for its billowing masses of crisp, clean, fragrant blooms.

Rosette de Lizy is a tea rose, one of a class of roses introduced into Europe from the Orient, It brought with it a high centered form and a good repeat bloom.

127

*Souvenir de la Malmaison is a
Bourbon rose named for the estate of
Empress Josephine. There she
attempted to grow every rose
available at that time.*

Mme. Alfred Carriere is a Noisette rose of unknown parentage and, like others in its class, it has full, large, very fragrant flowers that grow on a vigorous but tender climbing plant.

Like the Biblical rose for which it was named, the climber Joseph's coat, is a vibrant mixture of yellow, orange, and red colors that continually change.

There are few views more inviting than an arbor of climbing roses and clematis.

Harsh corners and straight lines are softened and interest added to windows, doorways, and eaves with the massive blooms of climbing roses.

The soft yellow buds of the floribunda Summer Fashion open into flowers of ivory and delicate yellow with rose-pink margins bordering the outer petals.

Like most mauve roses, the floribunda Angel Face is fragrant. Its ruffled deep lilac blooms will reveal a bright yellow center when the flowers are fully opened.

The large flowers of Kiss of Fire are soft yellow and perfectly formed; the edges of the petals are kissed by brilliant red.

The fragrant flowers of the floribunda French Lace are at first touched with soft pink and apricot, becoming the color of ivory lace when the blooms are fully open.

Named for the famous hybridizer of floribundas just after his death, Gene Boerner is a floriferous plant with perfectly shaped flowers. Ironically, Gene Boerner didn't like pink flowers.

Lagerfeld is one of four roses in the French Designer collection that were selected by and named for famous couturiers.

The grandifloras were termed to describe roses with hybrid tea rose-shaped flowers and the clustering habit of floribundas.

Lagerfeld has high centered, fragrant blooms and is very weather resistant.

*Hybridized by William
Warriner in 1971, the hybrid
tea rose Pristine has pure white
petals that are gently blushed
with pink.*

*Aside from its thorns, the flowers
of Susan Massu are gorgeous:
light yellow to orange, shaded
with red, and very fragrant.*

*Soft and relaxed, Summer Dream is
a captivating vision of shell-pink
shades, with orange in the center
and yellow on the underside of the
petals.*

The miniature Dreamglo has brilliant white and red flowers that bloom profusely all summer, holding their color well. Excellent in the garden, Dream-glo's long stems make it a good cut flower as well.

The Latin name for the snapdragon, Antirrhinum, *is from two Greek words that mean snoutlike.*

The only spiked flower among the top 10 most popular annuals is the snapdragon, which comes in a rainbow of all colors except blue.

Snapdragons grow to a height of about three feet. They prefer full sun and moist soil.

The sweet pea, Lathyrus odoratus, *is a very old flower, with lovely, fragrant blooms.*

The original sweet peas were maroon and purple, but breeding has created many different-colored flowers.

Sweet peas are hardy, annual flowers and, although some varieties are heat resistant, they prefer temperatures on the cool side.

Borne on long, graceful stems, red sweet pea blossoms enrich an early summer garden.

Tulips have been divided into a
number of classes based on the shape
of their flowers and their blooming
time. Late to bloom, lily-flowered
tulips have long, pointed, outward
curving petals.

Squirrels are notorious for breakfasting on tulip
flowers. However, a planting of lily-flowered tulips
will not usually be bothered by these critters.

The Hybrid Darwin tulips have the classic, egg-shaped flowers, but so far only red, yellow, and orange blooms of this type are available.

Parrot tulips are cheerful and somewhat informal with large flowers whose petals are fringed, feathered, and sometimes twisted.

In the mid 1960's, Tiny Tim revived an old song that invited the listener to "tiptoe through the tulips." Another lyric from yesteryear immortalizes the good old days — "when you wore a tulip, and I wore a big red rose."

The viridiflora tulip Hocus Pocus is a magic combination of yellow and red. It is a type of Cottage tulip with a colored stripe on the outside of the petals.

Jockey Cap is a Greigii tulip that characteristically has striped or mottled foliage, warm toned flowers, and short stems.

*Tulip flowers can be stuffed with
salads for a light summer lunch,
and the central portion of the flowers
may be sauted in butter for a treat
tasting like asparagus.*

*A massed planting of tulips is excellent for a formal
garden.*

The zinnia is one of the most versatile garden annuals, with plants ranging from inches to many feet in height. The flowers vary from tiny button-size to huge, dinnerplate-size specimens and come in a rainbow of colors except blue.

Index of Photography

TIB indicates The Image Bank